Executive Etiquette

Executive Etiquette

by Chester Burger

THE MACMILLAN COMPANY

COLLIER-MACMILLAN LTD., LONDON

Library of Congress Catalog Card Number:
69-18810

First Published by Collier Books

The Macmillan Company
Collier-Macmillan Canada Ltd., Toronto, Ontario

Printed in the United States of America

Introduction

THIS BOOK IS INTENDED to make life easier for you in getting and holding your job. It's based partly on my own experience and observations over more than a quarter of a century. But mostly it's based on the more recent experiences of young men and women now in their first jobs.

Some of them love their work, and some of them positively detest it. Some are sophisticated; some are inexperienced. All are college graduates. Some have entered scientific and technical work, while others (usually liberal arts majors or business administration graduates) are involved in general administration and management.

Most have gone to work for large national corporations, simply because that's where most of the jobs are. But not all. Several of those who shared their experiences with me are employed by local banks, public utilities, and service businesses like advertising agencies.

There are many differences in their working environments, but there are also many experiences they've shared in common. Experiences where they felt discomforted because they didn't know the right thing to do in a particular situation. Where they didn't want to embarrass themselves or others by showing their ignorance.

I remember one painful incident from my own childhood. I was a high school freshman, not yet turned the ripe age of 15, and the faculty had arranged a tea for our class. Now it so happened that I came from a coffee-drinking family. I don't recall that tea was ever served in our home. So when they served cups of clear hot water, with a little bag resting on the saucer, I logically proceeded, in the calmest and most methodical manner, to attempt to tear open the tea bag and dump the contents into the water. It seemed to me a perfectly reasonable thing to do. But when one of the teachers explained that you don't tear the bag, you dip it into the hot water, my mortification was so great that I recall the incident as if it were only yesterday.

Yet how could I be blamed for failing to know what to do with a tea bag? It was a new experience for which I wasn't prepared.

Well, in the light of the passing years, the embarrassment over that tea bag doesn't seem so important. But a corresponding gaffe on your job can make a big difference, because your associates will form their impressions of you very early in the game. The wrong impression has a habit of sticking to you long after you've outgrown it. Without a doubt, these impressions of you will prove at least as important as, and probably more important than, the quality of your work, when it's time for the boss to consider you for promotion. So it's important to make the right impression.

Right away, let me emphasize that the "right" impression isn't the same as total conformity. You ought to do the right thing regardless of what anybody else thinks. I recall an incident when an executive recruiter was interviewing a high corporate executive for a still higher post in another corporation. The interviewer, with his own peculiar "understanding" of psychology, chose to tell the executive an obscene story to test his reaction. Presumably, the executive was supposed to take it all calmly and as a big joke. But despite the fact that a tremendous corporate plum was dangling in front of him, the executive picked himself up, excused himself, and terminated the interview then and there. (It was the interviewer's turn to be embarrassed, and he recommended the man for the job anyway.)

On another occasion, years ago, the public relations agency of which I was president represented the Bourbon Institute, the promotional arm of the bourbon distillers' industry. In the early years after the Institute's formation, it was financed largely by Schenley Distillers, and so one day I was escorted to meet the president of Schenley's for luncheon in his private dining room. It was not a pleasant anticipation for me. For one thing, the president was reputed to be imperious and high-handed. And for another, I rarely drink (I don't often enjoy the stuff), and I assumed drinks would be served.

Sure enough, before luncheon was served, the butler circled the table, taking drink orders. One executive ordered bourbon on the rocks; another, a whiskey sour. This one ordered a manhattan, and that one asked for a mint julep. I never knew that bourbon could be served in so many ways. Finally, the butler got to me; I was sitting on the president's left.

My moment of truth had arrived. It would have been easy enough to conform and to request a bourbon something-or-other. But I turned to the president, cleared my throat apologetically, and said, "If you'll excuse me, I don't drink. I'd prefer a Coke."

His answer was immediate and explosive. "Dammit," he said, "we hired you people to help *sell* bourbon, not to *drink* it." And that was all there was to it.

So the purpose of this book is not to urge you to conform. It's to encourage you to do the right thing, the considerate act, the courteous act. When you get into an unfamiliar situation, I hope you'll find this book helpful in suggesting how it might be handled. Then you'll decide what's right for you.

CHESTER BURGER

Chester Burger & Company, Inc.
New York, N.Y.
February, 1969

Chapter 1

YOUR FIRST INTRODUCTIONS

TWO WEEKS AGO you were hired. Today is the morning you begin work in your new position. You walked in at three minutes before nine, after having arrived early and killed time in the nearby coffee shop. The broad smile on your face masks a mixture of happiness and anxiety.

Your department head greets you warmly, congratulates you, and begins your first morning by taking you on a quick walking tour of the offices. "I'd like to introduce you to the people you'll be working with," he says pleasantly. So down the aisle he takes you, stopping momentarily in each doorway for a 30-second introduction. "Jack, I'd like you to meet Tom Johnson. He's joining us this morning. This is Mr. Glug. . . ." The man's name is lost in a splutter. You don't catch his name, and he doesn't know what you've been hired for.

"Pleasure to meet you," you say. Then you're in tow again, on to the next office and the next introduction. This time it's Mr. Connors, or was it Mr. Rowley?

You're not quite sure. The third person you meet is Miss Gibson; you're certain of that. A good-looking gal. Then on to Mr. Grossman, Mr. Myers, Mr. Mac-Leod, Mr. Somebody-or-other, and Mr. Er-what-was-his-name. By the end of the tour, you can't remember who's who.

What do you do then?

Well, don't be too embarrassed. You're the one new-comer, so everybody will remember your name. But people hardly expect you to remember theirs, especially the first time around. So the next time you have an occasion to talk with one of your new colleagues, simply say, "I'm sorry, but when we were introduced that first morning, I didn't catch your name." He'll tell you—willingly. Nothing is pleasanter to a man's ears than the sound of his own name.

But don't forget it a second time. The way to remember his name is to use it: "Mr. Antonini, I'll follow up on this right away." Write his name down on a piece of paper the minute you're alone. If you make a special point of referring to people by name when you talk with them, you'll find their names rapidly stick in your mind.

SHOULD YOU USE FIRST NAMES?

We're living in an informal period, in clothes, manners, and habits. One of those informal habits is the use of first names in addressing people. A young execu-tive in a large Indianapolis corporation told me that in his company, only the president was referred to as "Mr." Everyone else was Joe, Archie, Frank, Don, from his first day on the job. If everyone else in your office uses first names, certainly you should too. But there are a few exceptions. Always use "Mr." when addressing an older man, or your boss. This holds true even if they address you by your first name. If you are too formal, they'll take the initiative in suggesting you use their first names. Particularly in a new job, it's better to be too formal than too informal. Using first names without invitation can give the impression you're a bit too "pushy."

SHOULD YOU INTRODUCE YOURSELF?

After you've worked there for a few days, you discover that your department head introduced you to everyone but his boss. It was an unintentional oversight, for his boss wasn't around at the time. But a few days later, he walks into your area, busily engaged in conversation with an unknown guest. He looks straight at you, with a slightly blank look. This certainly isn't the time to introduce yourself, but you can nod a pleasant good afternoon. Then, the next time you see him alone, simply approach him and say, "Mr. Treadwell, I'm Bob Otterbourg. I'm the new production man here, and I just wanted to say hello." It would have been a pleasant gesture if he had first introduced himself to you, but there's nothing wrong with picking up the ball yourself and taking the initiative.

HOW LONG IS A LUNCH HOUR?

When lunch hour comes, you have another new situation to contend with and a question to resolve: How much time should you take? Is an hour too long? Believe it or not, in some manufacturing companies, the lunch hour for executives is tied by custom to the length of the factory workers' lunch hour; if they get 30 minutes, the executive can "safely" take 45 minutes. In other companies, no one considers it improper to take an hour and a half, particularly when you're entertaining a business associate at luncheon. In the advertising industry, where business over luncheon is a standard practice, two hours is customary.

Your best guide, therefore, will be the habits of others around you. That will tell you more than if you ask the question directly. But be sure to observe your peers; not your boss or the oldest employee in the office; time and status may have given them certain privileges you would be rash to claim for yourself. And at the very beginning of your job, it would certainly be prudent to limit yourself rigidly to one hour, regardless of what others are doing, perhaps even if it means excusing yourself from congenial company with the explanation that you think you ought to be back promptly for the first week or so.

Even if they kid you, or joke at your expense, it will avoid giving the wrong impression to the boss. Later on, after you've learned "the lay of the land," you can afford to join the gang. But not the first week on the job.

WHEN YOU HIRE A NEW MAN

When you recall your own first day on the job, you can appreciate the difficulties for a new man whom you've hired. Common courtesy suggests certain responsibilities which are all too commonly neglected. Your responsibilities include introducing him not only to your staff, but to the workaday routines which he'll need to know. It's a proven idea to prepare a brief checklist of vital information. One such list, given to new employees in a large Wall Street law firm, tells them:

1. How to use the telephone. (Do you dial 9 to get an outside line? Do you place your own long-distance calls? What records must you keep?)
2. Where to get office supplies when you need them.
3. Where to phone for lunch when you must eat "in."
4. When to go to lunch, and when you're expected back.
5. How to get a cup of coffee. ("The coffee cart comes around at 10 A.M. and 3:30 P.M. daily.")
6. How to adjust the air conditioning vents if it's too cold, or the radiator if it's too hot in your office.

And it includes a shiny key to the men's room.

When you take the time and effort to anticipate questions like these, you're demonstrating interest in your new employee. You also eliminate the embarrassment which he'd feel by asking such "stupid" questions. Yet they're not stupid at all; how could he know the answers unless someone tells him? That someone should be you.

These may seem like minor details, hardly worthy of mention. Yet a junior executive once told me he had suffered considerable anxiety on his first day in the office when he had to deliver some papers to a high executive. He located the right door, but found it closed. Should he knock and possibly interrupt an important meeting? (He finally decided to knock.) When there was no answer, he wondered if he should enter. (He did so. The executive was talking on the phone.) Should he leave the papers on the desk and leave, or wait for the executive to finish and hand them over personally? (The phone conversation seemed of a confidential nature, so he placed the papers on the desk and walked out, closing the door behind him.)

No great crisis, certainly, and a situation which could be, and was, handled with ordinary common sense. But when I heard this story, I recognized afresh what I had forgotten many years before: When you begin a new job, you are desperately anxious to avoid committing a *faux pas*. It takes little more than good intentions and a few moments of your time to help the newcomer avoid typically awkward and embarrassing situations.

JUST OUT OF COLLEGE?

Nobody finds it easy to begin work in a new position. Besides all the problems of office etiquette, there is, of course, the work itself. If you've newly arrived from college or graduate school, you may be starting with a slight chip on your shoulder. You've just spent a year analyzing complex business problems; you've had a rounded education (considerably better, possibly, than your boss); and here you find yourself doing what seems like menial and routine work. To defend your injured pride, you may find yourself telling the boss you're qualified for better things.

Please don't. Resist the impulse. He knows it as well as you. If you're good, he knows he'll have to give you more responsibility soon or you will become restless. If you say something to him, particularly after only a few weeks on the job, he'll probably conclude you have unreasonable expectations he'll be unable to satisfy. If you say nothing, and simply do your work well, he'll mentally decide you're adjusting very well to the business world. Isn't that what you want him to think? And isn't it true?

RETURNING FROM MILITARY SERVICE?

The normal problems of adjustment to your new job will be compounded if you're returning to civilian life from military service. Your habits, your dress, your manners, your ways of handling people must suddenly change dramatically and completely. For two or three years, it's been drilled into your crew-cut head that you address people as "Sir." Now, that must go; it's a mark of subservience which demeans you. If you were an officer or noncom, you've grown accustomed to giving orders and knowing they'd be obeyed. But just try it in your office, and see what happens. In 15 minutes, your secretary may be in tears, and others on your staff will be muttering, "Who does he think he is, Westmoreland?" The labor shortage being what it is these days, they don't have to work for you; it is fairly easy for them to get jobs elsewhere. Try military behavior in an office and you, more likely than they, will be looking for employment somewhere else.

The authority the company has given you is worth only as much as the willingness of your staff to accept it. It's remarkable how willing they'll be if you treat them with courtesy and a respect for their dignity. Like saying "Please." Like saying "Thank you very much." Like confessing "I don't know how these matters are usually handled. Could you help me?" Such simple courtesies will ease your way. And always remember, nobody expects you to know everything about your job. No one will think less of you for asking questions, particularly at the beginning.

Just the other day, I stopped in a nearby luncheon-ette for a quick sandwich. The service was terrible. The man behind the counter seemed confused (three times, he came to give me a napkin), slow (he didn't know where to find anything), and disorganized (he didn't serve customers in sequence). The long wait tried my patience. Finally, the woman next to me, equally im-patient, angrily snapped at him, "What's the matter with you?"

"This is my first day on the job. I began at eight o'clock this morning," he replied matter-of-factly. Everyone heard both the question and the answer. You could see the resentment dissolving, turning instead to an attitude of sympathetic understanding and amused indulgence. All because everyone there could under-stand his predicament. Your frankness and honesty in your first days on the job will prove equally valuable to you.

Chapter 2

WHATEVER YOUR POSITION, whatever your company, and whatever your industry, you're likely to spend a substantial part of your time on the telephone. Many people, including some you've never met and never will meet, will form their total impressions of you from your telephone voice. So it's worthwhile to consider your telephone image (even before the Picture-Phone arrives and makes that word a literal reality).

What image should you project over the telephone? The answer is: the same image you want to present to anyone who meets you in person—friendly, competent, businesslike. The impression you don't want to give is unfriendliness, incompetency, unbusinesslike behavior.

INCOMING PHONE CALLS

Let's start with your incoming calls. When someone phones you from outside your building, the first voice they hear is that of your switchboard operator, "Ajax Manufacturing, good morning." At least I hope they hear that. It immediately creates a friendly impression.

Your caller asks for you by name, and his call is put through to your secretary. She should answer your phone, "Mr. Johnson's office," not "Hello," which tells nothing. Some companies, including the telephone company itself, encourage secretaries to answer, "Mr. Johnson's office. Miss MacLeod speaking." I like this. It tells the caller that he's dealing with "a human being person, not an IBM card," as a friend of mine puts it. When your secretary identifies herself by name, her pride and sense of responsibility are stimulated, for she's less apt to be rude or careless if she knows that the person at the other end knows exactly with whom he's been speaking.

Let me add a personal observation: Secretaries usually directly reflect their bosses' wishes in their telephone manners, because it's inevitable that sooner or later the boss will overhear his secretary's conversation, or receive a comment from a caller. If a secretary is rude over the phone (I don't mean once, but regularly, for anyone can slip occasionally), it's because her boss is quite willing to tolerate her discourtesy. If she's pleasant, it's because her boss has set that standard for her.

Since an important part of your job is to make friends for your company and yourself, it would be a good idea to emphasize this to your secretary. Tell her you want her to be friendly to callers; that her job is to help them, not to irritate them.

SHOULD YOUR SECRETARY SCREEN CALLERS?

The caller usually asks for you by name without identifying himself, and that's where the most frequent discourtesy occurs, however unintended. Too many secretaries automatically reply, "Who's calling, please?" No matter how politely asked, it's an irritating question. It implies that if the caller isn't the right person (whoever that may be), your secretary won't let him talk with you. That's exactly what she intended to imply.

But as it happens, all too often the caller with the unrecognized name may be important to you. He may be a new customer or a new colleague. He might even be someone you never heard of, wanting to talk with you about a new job. These people hardly deserve to be screened out by your secretary.

Your secretary should find out who's calling you, so that she can announce the call to you. But there are better ways to ask the question. The best is a simple change, "May I tell him who's calling?" Those few words eliminate the idea that she'll screen out his call.

Such a reply also tells the caller that you're in. And if you wish to talk with him at that moment, you can do so. Of course, you make the most favorable impression when you're immediately available.

WHEN YOU DON'T WANT TO BE DISTURBED

But perhaps you don't want to be disturbed just then. You may be working on a project, or attending a meeting, or whatever. And you've told your secretary, "No calls, please."

Then she can tell a caller, "Mr. Johnson is in, but he's at a meeting right now with some people. May he call you back as soon as he's free?" That sounds a lot friendlier than saying "Mr. Johnson left word he can't be disturbed." (Translated, that means "Who the hell are you to disturb him?")

Other secretarial irritants are the queries "Of what

company?" and, the worst, "What is it in connection with?" Better not to ask the questions, but if they must be asked, she should say, "May I tell him your company?" "May I tell him what it's about?" Just a few words added, but they change the tone from irritation to friendly helpfulness.

MAKING YOUR OWN PHONE CALLS

Most of the time, I prefer to make my own telephone calls, simply because it's quicker and easier than asking my secretary to make them for me. My only exceptions are long-distance person-to-person calls where waiting may be involved. When the phone is answered, I usually say, "Mr. Moynahan, please. This is Chester Burger calling." It avoids the question-and-answer routine; his secretary doesn't have to ask me who's calling. If I happen to be calling someone who doesn't know me, and if I'm unfortunate enough to get one of the rude secretaries who asks "What is it in connection with?" (with no "May I tell him" added) I reply, "It's in connection with such and such. Mr. Moynahan and I haven't talked before, so I don't think he'll recognize my name. Would you be good enough to ask him to call me when he has a moment?"

If secretaries in your office customarily place calls for the executives (I think it's a pretentious custom), you should pick up the phone as soon as your secretary has asked his secretary to put him on. You shouldn't wait for him actually to answer before you're ready to talk. If he's higher in the corporate pyramid, or older, courtesy dictates that he not be kept waiting. And if he's junior to you, well, he already knows his status; don't try to impress him with your importance by keeping him waiting. Of course, you can avoid all these status problems by the common-sense solution of making your own phone calls.

PHONING FOR JOB APPOINTMENTS

When you're out of work, you'll find yourself doing even more phoning than usual. Particularly in a large metropolitan area, you'll seek appointments with prospective employers, contacts and friends. Many of them will be frustratingly difficult to reach, and you may find yourself asking their secretaries to call you when they return. It seems logical and avoids wasted phone calls. But don't do it. Speaking from the other side of the fence, I have found it most irritating to return from lunch and to receive a message to please call Mr. Freeman, a name I don't recognize. I call him and discover he wants to see me about a job. My mental reaction is, "If he wants to see me, why doesn't he call me until he gets me?" Maybe I'm being unreasonable, but I suspect that other executives react the same way. Why take the chance of irritating some unreasonable guy like me at a time when you want his help?

MAKING PERSONAL PHONE CALLS

Is it proper to use your office telephone for personal phone calls? The question is theoretical, because there's no known way for your company to prevent you from so using it. Ever since dial telephones were coupled with "direct outside dialing," (eliminating the need to ask the switchboard operator for a line), your management can't really tell how many of your calls are per-

sonal or business. The result is temptation. It drives
cost controllers to distraction. They've tried everything
to control the problem. In one office, the supervisor
placed a piggy bank on his secretary's desk and asked
everyone on his honor to drop in a dime for every
personal call. In another company, a rigid rule was
adopted against personal use of the telephones, and
coin booths were installed in every corridor. That failed
too, although the booths are still there.

A sensible approach to the question is to limit your
personal telephoning to reasonable limits. You'll be the
judge of what's reasonable, but the less the better.
Nobody can object when you phone your wife to tell
her you'll be a few minutes late in getting home. But
when your phone line is tied up to incoming business
calls by a long social conversation, that's bad office
manners. Sooner or later, someone will notice, perhaps
your supervisor who has been dialing you and getting
a busy signal.

The same rule holds for incoming personal calls. An
occasional call is considered acceptable, but make a
habit of it and the company telephone operators will
soon be aware. (Why are they so perceptive?) Or else
the secretary at the next desk who sometimes answers
your phone will comment, "That didn't sound like a
business call to me." An executive I know told his wife,
"Never call me at the office unless it's a real emergency. An emergency is not when you overcook the
roast beef."

Chapter 3

COURTESY—AND YOUR CORRESPONDENCE

EVERY COMPANY KNOWS that your correspondence is a very important ingredient in determining its reputation in "the outside world." Many companies prepare correspondence manuals suggesting how to write effective letters; some companies even give courses on the subject. The only trouble is that all too often they give the manuals and the courses to the secretaries, not to the man who writes the letters. You.

I'm not going to try to distill these entire manuals into a few paragraphs. Besides, they're mostly concerned about effective communications, while I'm primarily concerned here with your good manners, as they show themselves in your letters.

Certainly, there's a need for courtesy in correspondence. Don't take it for granted; too often, it's absent. Last year, a very high government official wrote a personal letter, individually typed, addressed, and signed, to 2,000 presidents of U.S. companies, asking cooperation on a government project. Only some 43 of them had the courtesy to reply with either a yes, no, or maybe answer. The others didn't even respond!

Now if that's the way corporate presidents answer their mail, just imagine how executives down the line treat their correspondence! And if a high government official, a nationally known figure, is ignored in this discourteous fashion, where does that leave an ordinary member of the public, or one of your customers, when he writes your company?

You should answer your mail. If people go to the effort of writing you, even if to complain about something, they're entitled to the courtesy of an answer, even if your reply is only a couple of sentences.

ANSWER YOUR MAIL PROMPTLY

You should answer your mail promptly. Nothing makes a better impression than a prompt reply, for it shows, to use a trite phrase, that you care. With the current state of postal delivery in the United States, it may take a week for your reply to be delivered; that's all the more reason why promptness is called for. I believe you should answer every letter no later than the day after you receive it. If you need additional information before you can respond, it's certainly permissible to delay your response a few days. But if the delay is likely to be a week or longer, a brief note can acknowledge the letter and explain that you'll answer it as soon as you can get the necessary information.

If you're on a lengthy vacation for two or three weeks, your secretary can acknowledge the letter with a brief note explaining that you'll reply on your return from vacation after such-and-such a date. This isn't necessary, but it's a considerate thing to do.

Chapter 4

BUSINESS LUNCHEONS—AND WHO PAYS

YOU MAY BE one of the many fortunate executives whose duties require the occasional entertainment of business associates, suppliers, or customers at luncheon. Whether or not you've been given a credit card along with your key to the executive washroom, the rules of common sense still apply.

The first rule is that the host is expected to pick up the check. If he asked you to lunch, he picks up the check. If you've invited him, you pay. Just as simple as that.

Rule number two: If he's a supplier, if the implicit purpose of the lunch is to sell you something or to dispose you favorably toward his company, he picks up the check.

Rule number three: If you and your companion are business associates engaged in matters of mutual interest, you take turns in paying when you lunch together. The courteous thing is neither to impose on his goodwill nor to allow him to impose on yours.

Above all, don't argue about the check. If he reaches for the bill, let him—if he should. Maybe your conscience will feel better if you say, "O.K., but next time, it's mine." (Then do it next time.)

If you should properly pay for the luncheon, then promptly pick up the bill when the waiter leaves it. Or better still, discreetly signal the waiter with a pointing finger that you want the tab. If your companion insists, I'd simply say, "No, *I* invited *you.*" Usually that ends it.

Out of your wallet comes your Diners' Club, American Express, Carte Blanche, The Everything Card, the Cash-Is-Nothing Card, or whatever. The usual procedure is to write across the luncheon check "Service" and an amount equal to about 15 per cent of the total. Then sign your name. While you're finishing the second cup of coffee, the waiter will return with a ball pen and the appropriate form. On this, your tip has already been written. You sign again, and he proceeds to give you one copy of the credit card bill. I'd suggest that when you return to the office, you file the slip carefully, because the Internal Revenue people have a habit of coming around a year or so later and asking, "Why did you claim this as a tax-deductible expense? Whom did you take to lunch, and what business did you discuss?" At that point, you had better have a copy of your slip with a notation of whom you entertained, and even a few words about what you discussed—"sale of new equipment," etc. If you don't, and the company's claim of business expense is accordingly disallowed, it won't endear you to your superiors. The responsibility of keeping the record is yours, not theirs.

TALKING BUSINESS OVER LUNCHEON

Now, just because the luncheon must have a legitimate business purpose to qualify as a tax-deductible expenditure by your company, it doesn't mean that you must talk business from the moment you sit down. Assuming you invited your guest because you wanted (for perfectly proper business purposes) to win his goodwill or to convince him to buy your product or service, the customary procedure is to open the luncheon conversation with social chatter. It might be about his interests, yours, vacations, or whatnot. Anything but business. Then after a couple of drinks, when he's halfway through the entrée, you're supposed to swing into the business matters as gently as possible. He's supposed to be a bit surprised and a great deal interested. After all, haven't you warmed him up with your hospitality and sparkling conversation?

If that's the way you do it, you have good company. Most everyone does. I won't guess the number of business luncheons I've had which were played from the same script.

But is it the best way? Don't you really think friend Steve knows why you've asked him to lunch? Don't you believe he expects a business conversation, a proposal, an approach from you? And isn't it likely that he has at least some modest degree of interest—even without knowing the specifics—or he wouldn't have accepted? (After all, he *can* afford to buy his own lunch.)

So why not drop the pretense that deceives no one? Why not after a drink, or even two, tell him you have a business matter to discuss before going on to other things? You don't have to do it abruptly. You can listen to stories of his vacation fishing trip before getting started. All I'm suggesting is that after a reasonable interlude, you tell him you have a business matter to discuss and you'd like to dispose of it before going on to other things. You may be pleasantly surprised to discover that he'd rather dispose of it first too. You'll have more time to discuss the subject properly; your friend won't have to hurry away to get back to the office. And if you finish the business at hand and want to go on to talk of miniskirts and microskirts, well, go right ahead.

ARRANGING A LUNCH DATE

Sometimes you'd like, for business reasons, to meet a customer or colleague you've known only by mail or telephone. Lunch seems like a good opportunity to get acquainted. This situation calls for subtlety of expression. If you say, or write, "Let's have lunch one of these days," probably nothing will happen.

But if you say, "Let's have lunch one of these days. Does your calendar have any open spaces the week of the twenty-third?" You'll get action. Pinning it down to a definite period of time means that he'll certainly respond. If he doesn't want to lunch with you, he can still exit gracefully. But if you ask for one specific date, and he has a prior appointment for that day, you may lose your chance.

If he accepts and you work out a definite date, then the responsibility is yours to make a luncheon reservation at a restaurant of your choice. (It's hardly polite to keep your guest waiting for a table when you know in advance he'll be coming at a specified time.) Your consideration is a thoughtful gesture which he'll note and appreciate.

SMALL TALK

Many a young executive has told me, each as if he were the only one who ever had faced the problem, that when he went to lunch with the client or even with the office gang, he found difficulty in making "small talk." If only his other problems could be as easily solved!

Small talk can concern anything except the business matter at hand. It serves the useful purpose of enabling two people to get acquainted in a preliminary way; to judge the scope of each other's interests. There's nothing wrong with engaging in small talk—unless that's all you have to discuss.

But you need something to talk about, and it must come from somewhere. I remember from my college days a professor of constitutional law, a bachelor, who thought he had solved the "small talk" problem quite nicely. He fancied himself a gay blade, if not a young one. I recall his telling us that when he went out on a date, he carried two 3 x 5 cards in his pocket. One was a compilation of interesting and unusual facts he had gleaned from recent reading. He'd use these to make conversation, and presumably to impress his lady friend with his wide learning. The other card contained facts about her which she had dropped in casual conversation on previous dates, such as her food preferences, her likes in music, art, etc. Use of this latter information would presumably demonstrate his great attentiveness.

I was appalled. Thinking about it now, 30 years later, I can only decide that he must have been very dull companionship. If he needed index cards to remind him that shipments of canned kangaroo tails from Australia declined last year, something must have been wrong with the man.

Small talk can be based on your hobbies, recent books you've read, things you've done, people you've met, the latest news, your recent vacation, almost anything. If you're alive, you have the basis in your head for small talk. Unfortunately, not everyone is really alive. I know at first hand of one corporate executive whose interests were so narrow that he never read, never did anything (except lie in the sun on vacation), wouldn't look at a morning newspaper. His only amusement was watching Westerns on television—in glorious color.

What this fellow did with his time was his business, but it was, to understate, painful to meet with him or, even worse, to have lunch with him. He had absolutely nothing to say about anything, so he'd plunge abruptly into the business matter, and when that was done, excuse himself with equal abruptness. He neither knew, nor did he want to know, anything that was happening in the outside world.

WHEN TO PLAY THE SILENT ROLE

While you're becoming accustomed to handling small talk, occasional lapses may arise in your conversation, the deadly pauses that seem to you like five minutes (but more likely are closer to five or ten seconds). It's good to remember that the man you're talking with is interested in another subject even more than in you: himself. The best "small talker" I know is a man in his late thirties who can talk about almost anything, but he rarely does. Instead, he's always ready with a question for his companion: "What are your vacation plans this year?" "Have you been doing anything with your camera lately?" "How are your kids coming?" And so on. It works. A couple of questions like that, and your table mate may talk himself through a five-course luncheon, and leave convinced that you are the wisest of men.

Remember that you don't have to do too much talking. Think of how badly the other fellows want an audience! When they talk about their golf score, or their boats, or their hobbies, or whatever, you can get along just fine if you do nothing more than provide an attentive audience and ask the right questions at the right time. This will give you an opportunity to catch your breath, get acquainted with them, and get you off on the right foot. There aren't many good listeners these days; perhaps there never were.

And when the listening stage is past and the time comes when you feel more comfortable about contributing to table talk, be discreet in your own remarks. Approach certain subjects with great caution, or don't approach them at all.

Politics is one. If you can talk about it with calm moderation, fine. Go ahead. But if you feel a burning urge to damn the incumbents violently and convince your colleagues to see things your way, hold it. You are probably wasting your breath, and you are certainly opening the door to unforeseen animosities. The stronger your feelings, the more certainly this is so. If the fellow in the next office doesn't see things your way, no great harm has been done. But if he pegs you in his mind as something of a fanatic, you've damaged your reputation in his eyes.

The worst and most offensive case of this sort I ever saw happened in the late afternoon on November 22, 1963. A New York corporate executive had stopped into a nearby bar after lunch when the radio flash came that President Kennedy had been assassinated. Before the impact could sink in, he reacted in a manner to which his political beliefs had inevitably led him: he stood up and danced a quick jig, delighted that his personal villain had been removed from the scene.

The others present were shocked. As they realized the enormity of the Dallas crime, they became increasingly upset about the behavior of their colleague. The incident was duly and distressingly reported to his superior, and before five o'clock that afternoon he was fired. His boss was appalled by his bad judgment, offensive behavior, and by the volcano of repressed emotion which apparently lurked within him.

Discussion of politics isn't the only subject on which moderation (or silence) is indicated. Race and religion are others. You can be filled with prejudice (I hope not) but if you don't show it outwardly, who will know? It never was right, but it isn't in style these days either. The anti-Semitic sly jibe, the anti-Catholic remark, cruel references to Italian-Americans, and all the rest simply don't belong. Nor do anti-Negro or other racist "jokes" have any place. They hurt people, they mark you as a bigot, and they will not be taken kindly in an environment made up of people of many different ancestries. If some private hates lurk within you, the best thing is to get rid of them. The next best thing is to keep quiet.

Chapter 5

WHY YOUR DRESS IS IMPORTANT

YOUR PERSONAL BEARING, appearance, and behavior are important in your business life. Just as you take notice if your friends wear poorly tailored suits, or loud ties, or ankle-length socks, or unshined shoes, your supervisors notice your own dress.

These are superficialities, of course, but clothes tell much about the man. You have little excuse for careless grooming, for if you work in a corporate office, your salary should be adequate to provide decent dress.

I think you can tell the difference between an inexpensive suit and one which has been carefully made and carefully fitted. The latter is worth the difference in price. It's important because you want to create the impression, by your appearance as well as by the quality of your work, that you're right at home in the executive suite. Tasteful clothes, however, aren't the only thing; it's how you wear them. Even a fine suit will do your appearance no credit if the sleeves are wrinkled at the elbow and the pants unpressed.

Styles change with the times, but the requirement for good taste in clothes remains. What is good taste? It's up to you to decide. Only a generation ago, Thomas J. Watson, president of International Business Machines Corporation, required that all male employees wear a white shirt. Failure to conform was grounds for dismissal; you weren't the "IBM type." Today, IBM's sensible rule is, wear whatever you please, but be sure you're dressed tastefully.

What does that mean? It means clothes that are reasonably in style: no extreme fashions. It means no ostentatious colors, or overconspicuous jewelry that attracts attention to itself. It means socks long enough to cover your legs when you are sitting. And it means shoes that are well shined.

It takes a fashion expert to know when you're properly dressed, and I'm not a fashion expert. You can, however, get plenty of free advice from your local haberdashery or clothing store. It's their business to know. And with their sure help, you'll be able to concentrate your efforts on your work performance instead of suffering anxiety about your appearance.

SHOESHINES IN YOUR OFFICE

In some cities, shoeshine men regularly go through major office buildings, having acquired, by custom, or by cash, the privilege of walking into individual offices to solicit business. If one arrives while you're meeting with someone, and you need a shine, courtesy dictates that you invite your guest to have a shine first (at your expense). If he offers to pay, I'd say, "No, when I'm in your office, you pay. In my office, you're my guest."

GOOD POSTURE—GOOD IMPRESSION

If your posture is poor, and you slouch in your chair, you're not making the most of your appearance. Take the example of a tall woman, a really tall woman, say, over six feet in height. Such women are understandably self-conscious of their height. Some try to hide it by slouching into poor posture; others walk especially erect and tall. For one, her height is a liability; for the other, an asset. This makes the point. It may be difficult to break a habit of many years, but you'll find that good posture helps build the impression around the office that you're alert and on your toes.

A pleasant impression, based on careful grooming and good posture, tells everyone, including the boss, that you have pride in yourself. "I like to see a man proud of the place in which he lives," Abraham Lincoln once said. I like to see a man proud of himself.

Being proud of yourself isn't the same as trying to pose as somebody you're not. Affecting pretentious speech, phony accents, and the like, suggests to me that instead of being proud of yourself as you are, you would rather be someone else. You can't pull it off successfully, so why try it in the first place?

SMOKING ON THE JOB

Your smoking habits, if any, contribute also to your appearance. When you're working alone in your office, it's your private concern whether, how, and how much you choose to smoke. But when you're with others, consideration for them should influence your smoking habits. For instance, if your office is smoke-filled, it suggests that either your air conditioning is off when it should be on or you're smoking too much, or both. If you're dictating to your secretary, don't complain about the cigarette dangling from her lips when one is hanging from your own. More than one secretary has complained to me about bosses who blow smoke in their faces, or whose diction is difficult to understand because of a cigarette or (in my own case) a pipe clenched between the teeth.

The smoker, even the occasional smoker, finds his greatest need to light up during moments of anxiety. Such a moment is always a job interview, or an important meeting with his supervisor. This is the very moment when I would try hardest to avoid smoking, even leaving the pack behind me to avoid temptation.

The reason is to avoid *showing* signs of nervousness. You can be practically beside yourself with anxiety, but if you don't show it externally, nobody, including the boss, will know what's in your head. But you can hide nothing if you're puffing away hotly. The frequent short puffs and the dense smoke cloud signal to him that you're tense. It's not an image that builds confidence in your ability to handle difficult situations. Your doctor has his own reasons for wanting you to stop smoking; my additional reason is simply to help you protect your image in difficult situations.

THE UNCONSCIOUS CLUES THAT REVEAL

The trained observer can learn much about what's in your mind from outward signs of which you're usually unconscious. For instance, if you're being interviewed, and you find yourself unable to look the interviewer straight in the eye, it's a pretty good clue that, for reasons of your own, you're angry at him, even if you're not aware of it. The interviewer may not be fully conscious of your evasion, but most certainly it will affect the tone of your meeting, to your detriment. I'm not sure you can force yourself to look someone straight in the eye when your unconscious mind won't let you, but I think it's worth a good try. This doesn't mean staring at him constantly, but it does suggest that frequent direct looks will help you two "get on the same wavelength." There are many kinds of effective communication, some without words, and this is one of the most powerful.

You may give another clue to a perceptive observer by the tone of your voice. I don't think you can consciously control this. If you're in a cheerful, pleasant mood, your voice will have a certain "sparkle." But if you're depressed, angry, or unhappy, your voice will inevitably and invariably drop in tone, sounding low and flat. This mood too will convey itself to your interviewer. If you're in that kind of a mood, it would be worthwhile to try to make a special effort to compensate.

CONTROL—OR CHANGE—YOUR MOOD

Moods are contagious. If your mood is pleasant, self-confident, and assured, you will most certainly convey this feeling to your supervisor. You may even find his mood changing in response.

If your mood, at the moment, is one of anxiety, above all try not to show it. A good friend of mine, a highly respected senior executive in a conservative Boston corporation, faced this problem and handled it very badly. Perhaps you can profit from his example.

His anxiety, wherever or however it originated, certainly didn't arise from his actual situation. Within a period of two years, the company had increased his salary from $18,000 to $29,500 and promoted him to a vice-presidency. When he expressed worry about holding his job—less than five weeks after his latest increase—I therefore could accurately discount his fears. He even told me that the president had recently complimented him on his work.

Yet there he was, worried to death he'd soon be out of work, and where would he find a position at a comparable salary? I couldn't convince him that his fears were totally unjustified, for his fears apparently came from youthful experiences which had no relationship to his circumstances today.

His inner suffering was bad enough. But even worse was the damage he did to his position by revealing his fear to others. One day, for instance, he took a colleague (another vice-president) to lunch, and said, "Fred, I want to ask you a favor. Can you tell me how you think I stand around here? Do you think my job is in any danger?"

Up to that point, Fred had never considered that my friend's job might be in danger. In fact, he admired his self-confident manner. But after this unabashed display of "the willies," Fred began to eye my friend differently. Instead of strength, he saw weakness. And quickly, he found ways to capitalize on it to his own competitive advantage, and to the disadvantage of my friend.

How unnecessary it was! Fred, like most people, hadn't seen the clues in the worried look on my friend's face, and would never have known if my friend hadn't told him so. A good rule to follow is: If you're not sure whether to say something, don't. Share your anxieties with your wife, or with your personal friends, but never, never to a colleague on the job.

"FISHING FOR COMPLIMENTS"

Your anxiety can show itself in many ways; each of them should be anticipated—and prevented. One of the commonest symptoms is what I call "fishing for compliments." When you fish for compliments, you ask your boss or colleague a question which you hope will be answered by a compliment. Like, "Mr. Robertson, how was that report I gave you last week?" Or, "Joe, did my memo give you the answers you wanted?"

Obviously, you haven't asked the questions with the expectation of receiving criticism. You're hoping for a compliment. And you need one badly, right at that moment, or you wouldn't have asked the question. We've all done this at one time or another; unfortunately, I've done it too many times myself. But don't. Because it clearly signals to your superior that you're insecure and need a compliment. Once again, if you don't show insecurity, nobody will know you are insecure, regardless of what's inside your brain.

THE MEANING OF COMPANY LOYALTY

When executives are evaluating their staff, they invariably seem to consider an intangible element which they like to label "company loyalty." Mention of this term often elicits derision from the staff. "They're not buying me; they're buying my time eight hours a day," is a reply I've often heard.

Because I think the concept is as sound as it is misunderstood, I'd like to define company loyalty as I understand it, and as it applies to executives, junior and senior alike.

It does not mean that your soul belongs to the company. It does not mean you're expected to work night and day for the company. It does not mean that you're expected to put the welfare of the company ahead of your obligations to your family. It does not mean you're expected to swallow injustices done you by the company.

It does mean that while you're working, you make an honest effort to do the very best you can; that you take your work seriously. It does mean that you make a conscientious effort to be present on time, and to be available when needed if unforeseen contingencies come up. It does mean that you avoid talking against your employer on the outside. And it does mean that you make a serious effort to seal your lips to prevent accidental (or deliberate) disclosure of company secrets to outsiders.

KEEPING COMPANY SECRETS

My management consulting work brings me into contact with dozens of corporate executives each week. At social gatherings, I am frequently appalled by loose talk about company problems, new products under development, and new marketing plans, information that competitors would dearly love to know. The tone and manner of the speakers suggest that they are no more discreet at home on a Saturday night, or when sitting over a bar after work. Disclosure of unauthorized information can be so utterly damaging to a company these days that many companies have established elaborate security educational programs to prevent it. An important part of the concept of company loyalty is the protection of the company's business secrets.

Particularly in a smaller city, where economic life is dominated by a few major plants, social circles are smaller than you may sometimes realize. An indiscretion committed at one party may be repeated at another, and before you know it, your top boss hears that Jesse Randall has been saying the company is having trouble with its new Model 37 bulldozers. That isn't going to help Jesse Randall any.

You may feel a real need to unload some of your frustrations. If you do, share them with one close friend, a man you can trust implicitly. Don't go beyond that. That's part of company loyalty.

Chapter 6

JUST BEFORE NEW YORK's new Metropolitan Opera House opened in Lincoln Center, the vast stage turntable collapsed during a rehearsal. In the resulting disruption, the opera staging had to be changed, and several years later, the turntable still hadn't been rebuilt because of its huge cost.

They traced down the cause: the stage was overloaded. When they looked up the specification sheets, they found that the builder had been told to build for a maximum weight of 10,000 pounds. He had done so. But the stage managers who provided the specifications didn't realize that 10,000 pounds was the weight of only 50 people on the vast stage.

"It was my fault," said the man responsible. "Ten thousand pounds seemed like a lot. I should have checked."

And because of his honest candor, everyone understood that they too could have made the error. They sympathized with him, instead of blaming him. He remained in his post, as indeed he deserved to, despite the $150,000 magnitude of his mistake.

WHEN YOU MAKE A MISTAKE

Since you're a human being, as well as an executive, sooner or later you too will make a boo-boo, a damaging error that will cost your employer money and cost you considerable embarrassment. No matter how high your batting average, I'm sure it isn't 1000. So one day you'll suddenly discover that one of your plans went wrong, or that you shouldn't have approved something you did approve. And you'll panic inwardly for fear of the consequences.

If I can safely assume that you're generally thorough and careful, let me hasten to assure you that, somewhat surprisingly, your job will not be endangered, provided you handle yourself properly.

The first thing to remember in such a moment of crisis is, don't lose your cool. Don't panic. I'm reminded of a recent incident which occurred to the road company of the theatrical play *The Odd Couple.* The stage action called for actor Dana Andrews to remove his pants on stage, and day after day, he did so routinely. One day, a roar of audience laughter revealed he had forgotten to wear undershorts. Andrews didn't realize what had happened. Very calmly, actor Eddie Bracken turned to him and said, "You'd better put your pants on. We're expecting company." Andrews recovered his trousers and his equanimity quickly, and the play continued without a hitch. That's keeping cool when lesser men would have panicked.

So don't conclude that the world (or your job) will come to an end because of your mistake. The best course is to go straight to your supervisor, tell him you made an error, and explain in detail what happened and why. Don't evade responsibility; don't give excuses; don't minimize the consequences. Simply tell him the facts honestly, and apologize.

You'll come off best if you go to your boss first, even before he's heard the bad news. But if he hears it first and calls you in, the best course is, once again, to tell him the whole truth frankly and candidly. Be sure, also, that you tell him what actions you'll take to prevent a recurrence. After his initial anger, the overwhelming probability is that he'll tell you he understands, and not to feel too upset about it.

If you're still skeptical that your own error won't cost you your position, look at the case of Egyptian prime minister Abdul Gamel Nasser. In six days of war with Israel, his armies were scattered and broken; his equipment lay smashed and upturned in the desert. He was the commander-in-chief, and he was responsible. Yet when he went on Cairo Radio and publicly accepted full responsibility for his country's defeat, the Egyptian people rallied around him, refused to accept his resignation, and supported him totally. How different it would have been had he attempted to blame someone, anyone else! Isn't there a lesson here for the corporate executive?

Chapter 7

WHY PROMPTNESS IS IMPORTANT

IN OUR COUNTRY, the first sign of business etiquette is promptness. When you have a two o'clock appointment, you're expected to be there promptly at two, not at five or ten minutes after the agreed-upon time. Your host has set aside the time on his calendar to see you; if you're late, you're suggesting by your action that you don't regard highly the value of his time. And when you're on the other side, receiving a visitor for an appointment, courtesy demands that you see him promptly. Once again, keeping him waiting is a sign of inconsideration and disrespect.

This isn't so in other countries, where time has a different meaning. In Venezuela, for instance, I was once kept waiting more than an hour, despite a definite appointment with a prominent businessman. At the end of the long wait, he invited me into his office quite graciously, and we successfully completed a business transaction. The only thing that kept me from losing my patience was the knowledge that this was standard practice in Caracas. I was the visitor, the foreigner, so his standards, not mine, had to apply.

But here, it's a different story. Once, more than a dozen years ago, I arrived at a New York corporate headquarters office to call upon a vice-president with whom I was doing business. The appointment was firm and definite, and I showed up in the reception room right on time. The receptionist took my card, phoned inside to his secretary to report that I had arrived. But nothing happened. I assumed that he was involved in a long phone conversation, so I remained patient while I read a tired copy of *Business Week* in the reception room. After 15 minutes, I politely asked the receptionist to remind his secretary that I was waiting for him. Once again she took the message, but nothing happened. After 35 minutes, the last ten of which were spent drumming my heel and my fingers impatiently, I got up, told the receptionist I was sorry, but that I had another appointment and would have to leave. Before she could phone again, I was gone.

This experience disturbed me. It had never happened to me previously. Had I done the right thing? I returned to my office, and waited for the expected phone call of apology. It never came. Finally, the next morning, I wrote a tactful note along these lines, "I'm sorry we weren't able to get together yesterday, but I assume something important came up to prevent it. Please let we know when you'd like to get together."

He never answered the letter. I never again heard from him. Which only proved he was an offensively rude man. It would be a pleasure to tell you that he was subsequently fired, but the truth is he remains a vice-president of his company to this day. His subsequent silence convinced me I had done the right thing in leaving when I did. Except that maybe it should have been sooner, perhaps after 20 minutes.

KEEPING AN OFFICE DIARY

To keep your appointments on schedule, you need an orderly appointment book, like the "Day-Timer." You'll find it helpful to enter all your appointments, and their location. Whenever I make an appointment, I always note the man's telephone number, in case for any reason I must later cancel the date on short notice. That makes it quick and easy for me to phone him and arrange another date. In my book, two full facing pages are allotted for each day, so I have plenty of space to enter notes on dates when reports are due, when to phone for follow-up action, and so on. If you don't know what you're supposed to be doing at a particular time, you can hardly be expected to be courteous about it. When I make an appointment, I usually note the subject of the meeting too, so that I can prepare myself mentally to "shift gears" between meetings.

SICK LEAVE—AND WHEN TO STAY HOME

Everybody becomes ill sooner or later—maybe only with a cold—and companies anticipate there'll be occasions when you aren't well enough to come to work. So they establish sick leave policies: They simply expect that you'll be unable to report to work for a certain number of days a year. In many companies, the number of such days is kept a dark secret for fear employees may abuse it.

Sick leave isn't the same as an extra vacation. You aren't entitled to it automatically. It's a privilege for use only when you actually need it. On one hand, you shouldn't use it as an excuse to stay home whenever you have a mild ache or pain. But on the other hand, you should stay home when your presence in the office would jeopardize the health of others.

In one large air-conditioned office in Detroit, in a company which I was serving as a management consultant, a young executive caught a severe cold. He was serious-minded and highly motivated. He took his work so seriously you'd think this giant corporation would come to a halt if he had to stay out for a single day.

On this particular occasion, so he told me, he felt miserable, complete with sneezes, coughs, running nose, and all the symptoms of the common cold. But his sense of responsibility to the company impelled him to come to work. Finally, on the second day, the man at the next desk came over angrily after one of his sneezing fits and bawled him out for his inconsideration in endangering everyone else. The air conditioning had spread his germs right across the office, and one other man had already caught cold. "Do you want everyone else to get sick before you stay home?" He was worried by his sense of responsibility; his colleagues were worried by his irresponsibility.

If you do become ill, call your supervisor promptly and tell him you'll be unable to report to work. You don't have to apologize, but you should give him enough information to judge the seriousness of your malady. If you expect to come in tomorrow, tell him that. If you're unsure whether your illness is serious, advise him of that. If your illness develops during the day, and may keep you out tomorrow, it would be considerate to tell him so. It's difficult enough to do without you for a day or more, but it's even harder when he hasn't been forewarned and had a chance to rearrange the work which must be done.

TIME OFF FOR PERSONAL BUSINESS

On rare occasions, you may need time off for urgent personal business. These may include moving to a new home or something of similar importance. In such cases, always ask your supervisor in advance for permission. Even if your company follows a generous policy on such matters, it would be wise to ask him, rather than tell him flatly you're taking the time off. If you ask him, he'll feel he made the decision; if you tell him, he may feel resentful that you gave him no choice. Bosses have a funny habit of wanting to believe they're making the decisions. Your supervisor is probably no different.

THAT WEEKLY VISIT TO A PSYCHIATRIST

Asking—and getting—time off from work for regular visits to a psychiatrist can be awkward, chiefly because of the amount of time required and because, even in this day and age, your office reputation might be damaged by the knowledge that you are undergoing psychoanalysis or receiving psychiatric care. (I've observed that people who are healthy enough to seek assistance in coping with their problems usually are more stable than those who "cope" through alcohol, or those who simply don't cope and make life difficult for themselves and those around them.)

Roberta Ryan faced this problem. She believed it was no one's business that she had a regular weekly appointment with a psychiatrist at 11 A.M. Wednesdays. With considerable trepidation, she brought up the subject at the time of her first job interview. After all other employment details had been discussed, she said quietly, "Now, there's one thing more. I have a doctor's appointment every Wednesday morning, and I would have to take time off for it. But I'll be glad to make up the time by working late, or whatever you prefer."

"That won't be necessary, Miss Ryan," the executive told her, "that's quite all right." And she never mentioned it again. I'm quite sure that her boss correctly assumed exactly what it was, even though she never spelled out the details. Nor should she have. If your boss is less understanding, I can only suggest that you try to rearrange your weekly appointment. But above all, resist the temptation to "tell all." It's really nobody's business but your own.

CHRISTMAS PARTIES—AND DRINKING

Christmas presents a whole set of social situations for the new executive. The office party, Christmas cards, gifts for your secretary. You want to do the right thing appropriate to the mood and the occasion. But not more. Christmas observances in the office aren't the same as at home, and you shouldn't attempt to make them so.

Office parties seem to be on the way out, although many still are held, usually on the last business day before Christmas. In those offices, they customarily begin at lunchtime with sandwiches, canapés, and liquor.

Now, if you're a one-drink man, or a two-drink man, whatever your limit is, stick to it. Nobody is going to fire you for getting overly high or even drunk at a Christmas party. But I've seen several careers halted suddenly at Christmas parties for that very reason.

You can pursue that pretty young secretary into an office to seek fulfillment of your desires (or fantasies). But don't assume someone hasn't noticed your absence, her absence, or the fact that both absences occurred simultaneously. Can you blame your boss for deciding that if you lack discretion under these circumstances, you can't be trusted with greater responsibilities that require the discretion you seem to have abandoned? A good rule is, what you do with yourself and your life privately is your own business. But when it's done publicly, you yield your right to consideration. And no matter how comely or shapely she is, it's hardly worth the consequences.

CHRISTMAS CARDS——OFFICE AND PERSONAL

Office Christmas cards are a big business these days, perhaps bigger than the sentiments they're intended to convey. Many companies maintain carefully updated files of recipients, clients, suppliers, etc. just to make sure that everyone who should receive their "warm sentiments" does so. So should you. But don't overdo it either.

Your supervisor should head your personal list, and maybe his supervisor too, if you have fairly regular personal contact with him during the year. And your colleagues, the men and women you work with regularly. So should your secretary.

If they haven't met your wife, it's proper to sign only your name to the card, and to mail it to their homes. If you've met his wife, then, of course, address your card to Mr. and Mrs.

When it comes to Christmas gifts for your secretary, remember that most companies these days give some sort of a bonus at Christmas, usually one week's pay. Although your secretary has served you faithfully during the year, she's done it, so to speak, as her official duty. Therefore, only a token gift is in order, to indicate your personal appreciation for her help.

I'm going to assume that at some time during the year, she's done something, however small, for your wife. Or perhaps she's merely talked to her on the telephone. If either of these circumstances apply, I'd suggest that you mark your gift card, "From Mr. and Mrs. Thomas Johnson." This makes it both more personal and less personal at the same time, and that's a good idea.

WHERE TO HOLD AN OFFICE MEETING

One of the basic rules of office protocol is that meetings are held either in the office of the man who calls them, or on neutral ground. When junior and senior are to meet, the junior goes to the office of the senior. He never asks the senior to come to his office. If the senior got up on the right side of the bed that morning and felt unusually secure, he might considerately go to the junior's office for the meeting. But he's never asked to go there. I know a vice-president in a top company who won considerable respect among his subordinates by the simple act of always coming to their offices for meetings; he never asked them to come to his. They regarded this as a courteous gesture of respect and appreciated it the more because it was so unusual.

The conference room is, of course, neutral territory. And sometimes it's the best place to hold a meeting. This is especially true if you're in charge of a project in which your supervisor is participating. It's tactful to ask him to the conference room instead of to your office. And your colleagues, particularly those whom you (or they) consider rivals for promotion, will feel more comfortable there.

RACE RELATIONS IN YOUR OFFICE

The winds of change which are affecting American life these days are being felt particularly within corporation offices. Racial barriers to employment are being lowered or even dropped. The law requires it; social custom is accepting it; and business is adopting it. So you may be surprised to find that the man in the next office is a Negro. Shock! You've known Negroes all your life: the delivery boy, the shoeshine "boy" (he's 53 years old, but everyone calls him "the shoeshine boy"). You may have known one or two black students in college, although you never got to know them well.

Now, suddenly, you find yourself working side by side with a black man as a social equal, at least in the office. Your sense of shock is compounded by your discovery that he's every bit as well educated as you and as intelligent as you; and, aside from his skin color, he's just like anyone else.

If you have the usual share of prejudices (they're hard to escape in twentieth-century America), you may be inclined either to give him the cold shoulder, or else to lean over backward to cultivate his acquaintance as a cover for your uneasiness. Neither is good manners. Symptoms of prejudice will reflect unfavorably upon you, and probably will hurt your career more than your behavior will injure him.

In your office work together your objective should

be to treat him exactly like anyone else, neither more nor less. The normal courtesies between executives are called for: a friendly greeting, polite conversation as with anyone else, a cooperative spirit when working together.

He doesn't expect you to be overly friendly, to be invited to your home, to share your social life, or anything else. He doesn't expect you to invite him to join you at lunch, unless you often lunch with others in the office. Again, a good rule is, treat him like anyone else and you'll have no problems. He wants to be judged as an individual on the basis of his own work, not as a member of a group.

This means that if you have occasion to have to criticize him for his work, you should criticize him just as you would anyone else. You don't do him a favor by holding back because of his race. But make your criticism (or better, positive suggestions) just as specific as you would for anyone else. Never talk to him as a member of a group. "You people . . ." is enough to make anyone's hackles rise. No matter how kindly intended, he'll be offended because you're saying to him, "I don't regard your primarily as an individual, but as a black man."

And when you find yourself talking with him over the luncheon table, a sound guide is to talk with him exactly as you would with anyone else in a similar position. If you'd normally talk about vacations, sports, or anything else, then do the same with him. Not that there's anything wrong with discussing race once in a while (it is a vital issue on the American scene, and he may have something interesting to say), but many Negroes do get awfully tired of talking about race with well-meaning whites. If you feel the urge to unburden yourself (The Great American Guilt Complex), then do it once and go on to other things.

Of course, there are cultural differences between races; how could it be otherwise? For example, it may well be the custom in your office to address your colleagues by their first names. Yet to many Negroes, this is an unwelcome familiarity, because they associate it with the Southern tradition of addressing all Negroes by first names, regardless of age or status. To this day, many men of color use only their first initials as a device to protect themselves against this insult. You might therefore find it wise to address your new colleague at first as "Mr. Johnson," at least for a few times, and then ask his permission to call him by his first name. You can be sure he'll appreciate your sensitivity to his feelings.

If you, the reader of this book, happen to be a member of a minority group, the same basic rules of good manners apply. If you want to be regarded and treated as an individual, then you have the responsibility of acting that way. Don't assume that every criticism and every action directed toward you is because you belong to a minority group. Perhaps it's an individual matter, directed to you as an individual, and perhaps equally, you can correct the conditions which brought on the criticism. It works both ways.

Chapter 8

GOING "THROUGH CHANNELS"

OFFICE ETIQUETTE IN every company requires that you go "through channels," that is, not over the head of your supervisor, nor directly to those who report to your subordinates. This policy is founded on solid ground. If, for example, you were to issue instructions directly to someone "in the ranks," you'd inevitably make life difficult for your own subordinate. You've given him the responsibility for his group, but you're exercising your authority to control them. Under the circumstances, you can hardly blame your subordinate if things go wrong. Long experience has demonstrated that it's best to issue your instructions through him instead of around him. This strengthens his authority over his staff, and gives him the freedom to carry out your instructions most effectively because he's closest to the people who will actually do the work.

WHEN YOUR BOSS BREAKS THE RULE

Problems arise, however, when your own supervisor doesn't follow this sound rule. You may discover, for instance, that while you were out of the office at a meeting, your boss asked one of your staff to help him immediately with a so-called urgent project. Maybe it was urgent and couldn't wait until your return, but on the other hand, postmortem examinations suggest that such projects are seldom as genuinely urgent as they're presented at the time.

The office pecking order being known to all, your subordinate immediately said, "Yes, sir," dropped the work you had assigned to him, and swung into action on the boss's request. What else could he do? What else would you have done?

But where does it leave you? Your assigned work has been delayed by the interruption. Your pride has been hurt ("I'm running this department, not he"). Your emotions run high ("I'd like to tell him off"). Once again, the usual cooling-off period should prevail. Don't make a move until you have all the facts.

First investigate quietly to determine if the project really was an emergency. It may have been. If it was, forget the matter right then and there, and cool off too. But if you find that the matter could have awaited your return, why not delay action for a few hours or a few days just on the off chance that your boss may call you in, tell you about it, and ask your understanding (if not your forgiveness)? Before you attack him with angry words, you may discover that he understands the problem as clearly as you. In such circumstances, you're expected to show friendly patience.

If a few days pass and nothing further is said, or, even worse, if it happens again, you might consider some corrective action. Your boss is the only one to discuss it with; not his boss or anyone else. And if we assume—it's a reasonable assumption—that he's more concerned with his problems than with yours, then you'll need to present the problem in terms which are important to him.

For instance, you might say, "Mr. Boettinger, I've got a problem. Maybe you can help me. You asked me to assemble that information you wanted, and to have it ready by tomorrow morning. But now Frank is working on the other project you gave him. Your other job has been pushed aside. I want to get it to you on time, and if you could let the work assignments go through my desk, you can be sure you'll get them on time."

With such a tactful approach, you accomplish several things. For one, you show him that *his* work will suffer from such interruptions. After all, this is what he's primarily concerned with. For another, you're asking for his help, instead of complaining. People like to be asked for their help, because the request implies a compliment (i.e., that they are qualified to help you). And best of all, you haven't complained or whined about usurpation of your authority, a subject that has rarely been known to elicit sympathy from a supervisor.

Your relationship with your supervisor becomes even more strained when your staff members report to you that he's been asking them about your performance. (Yes, this actually happens; in fact, quite often.) You worry about what they've told him; you recall you had occasion only last week to discipline one employee, and what did he say about you to your supervisor? And then there was that other incident. . . . You recall one after another. And worry. What can you do about it?

I'd do nothing and say nothing. Inwardly, you can only hope that your supervisor has good judgment and the ability to evaluate objectively what he was told about you, both good and bad. You can hope that he will assess you from other viewpoints as well: his own observations, your performance record, and so on. And perhaps he will.

You'd probably find it impossible to discuss the matter with him in a calm and collected way. Because his opinion affects you so vitally, you can hardly expect yourself to remain detached and unemotional. And because the subject may involve criticism of you, you can hardly expect yourself to avoid defensiveness. Better do nothing; say nothing, and hope for the best.

A touchy situation can arise when your supervisor asks you privately to report on the comings and goings of your associates. After all, your responsibility as an executive includes reporting on and supervising the work of others. It is quite proper for the boss to ask you to report on the performance of your staff. Supervising and reporting, however, isn't the same as informing. Your boss has a right to expect honest and complete evaluations of the people who report to you, but he has no right to expect you to snoop on them. Snooping is a distasteful role to most people I know, excepting only the few who like to play James Bond. I think it's a situation that's best avoided, because as I see it, your involvement can only do you harm.

You can hardly tell your supervisor, without offending him, that you don't want to do his dirty work for him. But you can find tactful excuses to avoid getting sucked in. If he asks you when So-and-so went out to lunch, you can tell him you didn't notice, that you were absorbed in your work at that particular moment. And so on. Three or four times in my working career, I've seen supervisors scold an employee on the basis of this kind of "private eye" information, and each time they would remark, "So-and-so saw you leaving at ten minutes to five." That will only create problems if Mr. So-and-so is you. The staff will avoid you like the plague.

So handle the situation gingerly, not eagerly. Try to avoid a head-on conflict with the boss. Don't let your disgust show; management will hardly develop trust in you if it feels you're identifying with the staff. Altogether, it's a delicate situation to handle without getting hurt.

BEWARE OF GIVING CRITICISM

When you evaluate the work of your staff, you'll usually find that their plans, proposals, or work performance deserve—and need—your criticism. But beware!

My observation, generalized over a lifetime of experience, is that people can't take criticism. Nobody. Not you. Not your boss. Not me. Not your wife. Not anybody. Just as flatly as that.

I didn't used to believe this was true. In my work as a management consultant, I witnessed many occasions where a company president politely—or not so politely—criticized one of his vice-presidents, who seemingly took it in good grace. But afterward, in private meetings with the vice-president, I quickly uncovered the vice-president's resentment, and was forced to wonder if anything positive had been accomplished.

HOW TO CRITICIZE PEOPLE—AND WIN

It's a difficult problem. Sometimes people need and deserve criticism. But if they resent it, what do you do then? One remarkable answer came in a motion picture production company, and I saw it at first hand.

The company had received complaints that many of the splices in its film prints came apart during projection. Because of careful record keeping, the management was quickly able to determine that one particular individual, whom it identified by name, was responsible for the careless work.

You would think that the department head would either call in the offending employee and criticize his work, or else would take the easy way out and call a meeting of all the film technicians in the group and generalize his criticism, asking all for cooperation.

But in this case, he did neither. He reasoned that if he criticized the offender, the man would resent it, become defensive, and as likely as not, express his resentment in more careless work. So the executive called a department meeting and said, "Gentlemen, we've been getting complaints that our film splices have been coming apart. This is causing a lot of trouble for us. I think the reason is that we're not using fresh cement. So from now on, let's use fresh cement every morning, and throw out what is left from yesterday. That should solve the problem."

A voice was quickly raised from the group. It was the known offender, the man who didn't know that he was known. "Fresh cement will help," he said, "but that's not the real problem. I think we've been getting careless. I know I have. We've just got to be more careful, that's all."

And he was. The complaints disappeared. The supervisor's plan succeeded.

It succeeded because he didn't criticize the culprit. And the offender, not being placed on the defensive by criticism, could afford to plead guilty and promise improvement. Quite a lesson, isn't it?

PUT CRITICISM IN POSITIVE TERMS

The lessons it suggests aren't easily learned. You can easily enough learn not to give direct criticism. To put things in positive terms instead. But what about the unintended criticisms that seem to "slip out"? What about the unintended hostile tone of voice, which says more than a dictionary full of words? When you feel hostile, it will probably show.

I'm not one of those who believe that when you're angry, the best thing to do is to "let it out." At least, not in the office. The consequences can be damning. As was written thousands of years ago, and is still true: "A soft answer turneth away wrath." It takes two to make an argument. If you criticize someone, he'll strike back, and there's your argument. If he criticizes you and you respond tactfully, that's the end of the argument.

One business acquaintance of mine here in New York has a standard response to criticism. No matter what the nature of the complaint, no matter whether he thinks it's justified or not, his reply is always the same: "You're right. That shouldn't have happened. I don't blame you for being annoyed. But there are some other facts we ought to consider. . . ."

He then goes on to give his justification for his action. He gives it as quietly and factually as possible. He tries to avoid an attitude of defensiveness. And he tells me—not at all to my surprise—that the matter is invariably dropped right there. By identifying himself with the opposite viewpoint ("You're right"), he removes his critic's disposition to argue further.

Well, if it's as simple as all that, why don't executives (or people in general) take criticism calmly? There are many reasons, and one of the most basic is that they lack the ability to see clearly why the other fellow is criticizing them. The reason may have nothing to do with them. Maybe he simply got up on the wrong side of the bed that morning and is angry at the whole world. Maybe someone has just criticized him. Maybe he's insecure in his job and reacts by hacking away at the people under him. Maybe he had a breakfast argument with his wife. Whatever the reason, it would hardly make sense under such circumstances to defend yourself or your actions. You might only succeed in giving him a target for his own hostilities and frustrations. In which case, watch out.

You may be unable to recognize or identify the real source of his anger. But if it's disproportionate to your alleged offense, give a soft answer along the lines my friend uses, and then disappear. When the boss is in a bad mood, stay out of sight.

MAKING THE MOST OF A COMPLIMENT

Many men seem to find it almost as difficult to take compliments gracefully as to accept criticism. I've attended many a sales meeting where the winners of a sales contest were announced, and all too frequently, the winner accepted his award with the grace of a bull elephant, acting as if he really didn't deserve it. Such gauche behavior embarrasses all concerned.

First of all, let's understand why your boss compliments you for good work, when he does. He's experienced and sophisticated enough to know that praise is the most powerful stimulant known for better work. (In fact, one researcher has found that even when work is unsatisfactory, a compliment is more apt to improve things than criticism.) Also, he feels good when he compliments you and receives your appreciation. He wants to be liked. Complimenting you buys your approval.

So don't spoil things for yourself and your boss by spurning or minimizing his compliment. Thank him for it, and tell him you appreciate it. Accept it in a generous spirit. If others shared in the work for which you're being complimented, let the boss know it. You'll look better in his eyes for it, not worse. For instance, you might say, "Mr. Winton, I'd like to tell Fred McWilliams and Mary Gibson about this. They helped me get this project accomplished, and I know they'll be happy to know you liked it."

The kind words of your supervisor, however, won't always be given to you face-to-face. More often, a brown interoffice envelope will contain a short memo, thanking you for an excellent job. If the boss happened to feel in a particularly philanthropic mood at the moment he wrote you, he's marked the memo for a copy to be sent to his boss up the line. It gives you a heady feeling.

Such memos are the stuff by which egos are built and maintained. One friend of mine always makes a few Xerox copies, writes on them, "Thanks for *your* help," and send the copies to the appropriate people on his staff before taking home the original to show his wife. It's a technique which makes friends and stimulates better performance.

WHEN YOU'RE PROMOTED OVER OTHERS

If your promotion has jumped you over the heads of other employees who have been in the department longer than you, you'll need a considerable amount of tact and skill to establish yourself firmly in your new position. People being what they are, the employees who were skipped over will hardly accept you graciously. Since your promotion represents an implicit criticism of them (for they weren't given the job), they'll convince themselves and each other that you won the race because of the boss's favoritism; in fact, any reason at all except that you're more competent than they. And they'll reveal their resentment by passivity and minimal cooperation. Their aim, of course, will be to decrease your effectiveness to make you fail, and thus prove they were right.

This is a common situation, and one best met head on. In fact, it's best to anticipate the problem even before it has a chance to arise. If you've just been promoted above one of your colleagues, why not make the first move, and make it tactfully?

For instance, you could ask him to lunch and bring the subject out in the open. You might tell him that you understand he's probably disappointed that he didn't get the promotion he had hoped for, and you appreciate his feelings. But since, "for one reason or another," they selected you, you're now going to need his help and cooperation in the department's operation. You're sure he'll give you this cooperation, and you in turn will do everything you can to treat him with the respect which his years of service to the company have earned.

In other words, I wouldn't ask him for his cooperation; the sheer act of asking will make you dependent upon him. I'd tell him, gently but firmly, that you need and expect his cooperation. That's a courteous way of establishing your authority at the same time you're paying tribute to his importance in the continuing operation of the department. If more than one person were similarly affected, I'd talk to each separately along the same lines. Of course, it doesn't have to be at luncheon. In fact, it might be better to talk with each in your office, one after the other, so closely in sequence that they can't compare notes between your meetings. And if this initial talk doesn't produce the results you want, you may have to do it all over again at the very next sign of noncooperation. In any case, don't let the incidents accumulate without acting firmly and promptly.

Chapter 9

TRADING SALARY INFORMATION WITH YOUR COLLEAGUES

LET'S TALK ABOUT money. I'd rather you talk about it with me than with your colleagues. Because such talk in the office always leads to problems, and almost never to getting you an increase.

The men in the factory know the hourly wage rates of every man in the plant, right down to the penny. These are usually matters of public record, specified in union contracts after public hassling and negotiation.

But there's a different tradition in the office. Executives don't discuss their salaries, because each is separately arrived at on the basis of the individual's experience, qualifications, length of service, and sometimes his bargaining power. Frictions will certainly ensue when you compare your salary with someone else's. If he's making more than you, you resent it—and him. If you're making more than he, *vice versa*. If you're both making the same salary, each of you will think you're worth more than the other. The discontent begins with the comparison.

How can you use this "valuable" information? If you go to the boss and mention it as an argument for a salary increase, you're asking for trouble. He may tell you, properly, in his opinion, that friend Jack is worth more to the company. That won't help your ego, and you may find yourself getting angry at your boss and at friend Jack too. Or the boss may tell you that Jack has been with the company longer, or has had more experience than you. Whatever he says, you're likely to construe it as a criticism; yet this is the boss's way of defending himself against your implication that he's been unfair.

My observation, based on inside knowledge of many companies over many years, is that you don't get raises that way. I'm not even sure you get them by asking for them in a positive way, even though I'll concede this sometimes may speed up the action.

HOW YOUR BOSS DECIDES ON SALARY INCREASES

Put yourself for a moment in the shoes of your supervisor. Once or twice a year, depending upon the custom in your company, he is required to review all executive salaries. Usually the personnel department provides him with a list of everyone in his department, together with their current salary, the date they joined the company, the date of their last increase, and the amount of their last salary increase. Along with this data sheet comes a budget allocation, indicating the total amount of money he may allocate among his staff. Let's say, for example, that his budget increase amounts to 5 per cent of the total department payroll.

As a starting point, he may pencil in a 5 per cent increase for each person, "just to see what it looks like."

Then he notes that Mr. Newsome has been doing an especially good job lately; "I'll give him another $10." That $10 will have to be subtracted from someone else's increase; "Oh, yes, Giardino has been slipping. Getting careless. In fact, he really deserves no increase. I'm not sure I'm going to keep him on." A mark of the pencil, and Giardino's $20 increase is gone. The boss now has $10 available to give to someone else. And so on.

But the people involved rarely see it like this. They don't always realize that the supervisor can't give out raises whenever he wishes and in whatever amounts he likes. Nor do they realize that the boss is guided by his total impression of each individual when he makes his decision; he rarely if ever sits down and reviews each man's work in detail. If his total impression is influenced by a complaining visit, the chances are considerable that you won't come out ahead.

HOW TO ASK FOR A RAISE

So how do you get a raise? There are three ways. The first is simply to do excellent work, and make sure the boss knows about it. In many companies, this is all you need to do.

The second method—I'm sorry to be cynical, but it's true—is to make the boss feel good. If he feels certain of your loyalty, respect, and admiration, he'll be more inclined to be generous.

And the third method, which is sometimes necessary, is to go in and ask for a raise. You should consider this only as a last resort, after everything else has failed, for the reasons I've already described.

But if you feel compelled to ask for a salary increase, here are some suggestions.

1. Don't give him the reasons why you *need* a raise. He's not interested. If you have "another mouth to feed," that's unfortunately or fortunately your problem, not the company's. Salaries are determined by the value of your services, not by the number of your dependents.

2. Don't be defensive. Don't try to build a lawyer's case to justify your request. For instance, a junior executive in one of the steel companies assembled a collection of complimentary memos he had received at various times. When he went in to ask for a raise, the memos came with him and were neatly deposited on his supervisor's desk as proof that he deserved the raise. It didn't work. The boss resented his pressure, and the man became immediately defensive over the quality of his work, citing the memos to prove its excellence. If your boss wrote the memos, it's safe to assume that he indeed knows your work has been good. Using his own memos as a weapon against him is neither necessary nor desirable as a bargaining technique.

3. Put your case in positive terms. Tell him the reasons why you believe your services are worth more to the company. Be specific, but also be careful not to exaggerate. If you played an important part in an important and successful project, it's certainly worthwhile to remind him of that. But if you claim responsibility for the success of the entire project, you may be overreaching yourself. Better understate than oversell.

4. Don't box the boss into a corner. If you push him too hard, he'll resent it. He wants to feel that he makes the decisions, not you. Let him know that you respect his fairness, and that whatever he decides, you know he'll do what's fair and best. (A compliment to his fairness is more likely to accomplish your objective than the suggestion that he's been unfair.)

IF YOU HAVE ANOTHER JOB OFFER

If you've already received a job offer from another company at a higher salary, don't play games. Before you go near the boss, decide what you really want. If you really want to stay, but the financial difference is substantial, tell him that. Say that if you possibly can get a reasonable salary adjustment, you would much prefer to stay with the organization, but the offer you have is so much greater than your present salary, you have little choice. And if he comes through with an immediate pay boost for you, don't then go back to the outside company and use it to try to negotiate still more. You might get away with it (although I doubt it), but the attitude of Company Number 2 will be that you've been using them as a lever to squeeze more money out of Company Number 1. Unless you happen to be the foremost missile scientist in the U.S.A., you're not likely to pull it off successfully.

On the other hand, if you have really made up your mind to leave your present company, and another organization has already made you a more attractive offer, be prepared to stick with your decision to leave. Unless your present employer comes through with a simply staggering increase (which is possible, but highly unlikely), don't change your mind and agree to stay. If you accept a modest increase and remain, the boss will, more than likely, resent you for having squeezed it out of him under duress. And when you return to Company Number 2 to tell them you've changed your mind and decided to stay where you are, you'll leave a bad taste in their mouths too. It won't help your future career, either way.

YOUR FINANCIAL RESPONSIBILITY

As time passes, and you rise in the corporate hierarchy, you will be given gradually increasing financial responsibility. At first, that responsibility may be limited to minor items such as your own petty cash and entertainment. Later, you may be asked to approve minor expenditures of other staff members; then, purchases of some equipment and materials, and so on. No matter what your job, therefore, your personal reputation for financial responsibility is important.

Companies assume, and I believe rightly, that if they're going to entrust you with their money, you should have demonstrated the ability to handle your own. They're not interested in your personal finances (and it's none of their business) unless irregularities in your personal funds come to their unavoidable attention.

One way this can happen, of course, is through garnishments against your salary. You've owed people money; they haven't been able to collect it, and they've gone to court and obtained an order to your employer to deduct a certain percentage of your salary each week and turn it directly over to them. Every personnel manager always has a few garnishments on the books. Now, it's bad enough when an industrial worker, who's perhaps making $125 a week gross salary, gets into debt over his head. But if you're earning perhaps $10,000, $12,000, or $15,000 a year, garnishments against your salary tell your employer that you're simply unable to handle your personal finances in an orderly and responsible manner. He probably won't discharge you if your pay is garnisheed, but the personnel man will most likely report it to your immediate supervisor. And your chances for further advancement probably will end right then and there.

I know a very pleasant fellow who's been deep in debt as long as I've known him, even while his salary hovers around the $18,000 mark. When he lost a job several years ago, he decided he'd have to "disappear" for 30 or 60 days so that creditors couldn't garnishee his salary until he had established himself in a new job. His curtain of secrecy lasted about that long; then they located him in his new company, "attached" as much of his salary as the law would allow, and they'll probably keep collecting, one little bit each week until the end of time, for it will take that long to repay the massive debts he accumulated. Fortunately, his employer didn't fire him, but made sure that he'd never have access to any company funds. Since that early moment, my friend has been on the defensive; he tells me he constantly fears that unless he does his work better than everyone else, they're likely to fire him quickly. Not a very pleasant way to live.

In another company, I know a young man whose salary is currently $12,500, but whose penchant for the "better" things of life suggests that he's living at a standard of living perhaps twice as high as his salary. A new car every year, tape recorders, hi-fi consoles, fine cameras, new suits, golf clubs, all seem essential to this man's happiness. He's not in debt, at least as far as his supervisor knows, and his salary has never been garnisheed. So where is all the money coming from? From his family? They're not wealthy. From kickbacks from suppliers? Maybe. The company has probed and been unable to find evidence. He's not talking. But it's coming from somewhere, and management is concerned. As I write this, they've already removed him from any authority over purchasing, selection of suppliers, or expenditures. And I'd be willing to bet he'll be out of his job by the time you're reading these pages. There may be nothing wrong with supplementing your income with family assistance, if you're lucky enough to have it available. But couple that with evidence of irresponsible spending, and why shouldn't management conclude that you don't know the value of a dollar?

ASKING FOR A SALARY ADVANCE

You may similarly damage yourself by asking for a salary advance. Of course, there are sometimes legitimate reasons: family emergency, serious illness, or an unexpected tax bill. If you have a good reason, and you need the money, a salary advance is sometimes preferable to making a bank loan. But ask it for a routine expense, or ask for it more than once, and you're telling the boss in clear tones that you're unable to budget your income, evidence of financial irresponsibility.

Chapter 10

ARRANGING YOUR BUSINESS TRIP

FOR SEVERAL WEEKS, a notation on your desk calendar has reminded you that a trade show is coming up in Chicago. It's a convention in which your company participates, and you know that several important customers will attend. In the back of your mind is the hope that you may be asked to go. Wonderful, exciting Chicago! Glamorous Chicago! You've never been there, and, in fact, you've never been sent out of town by your employer.

Miraculously, you get the word you're going. Two weeks before the event, your supervisor one afternoon casually says, "Oh, by the way, I'd like you to go out to Chicago for the show." "Yes, certainly I'll go," you answer, as if it were the most routine thing in the world.

But it isn't. It's a "first" for you. You don't know what arrangements to make, or who makes them. You don't know who pays for what, or how. Mixed with your excitement is a slight tinge of suppressed panic.

The first step is to ask your secretary to make plane

reservations. If it's a "first" for her too, she might begin by asking your supervisor's secretary how it's done. Some companies use a particular travel agent for all plane reservations; others prefer that you deal directly with the airline itself. Your company has a definite policy which should be followed.

Normally, all business travel is done tourist class, but there are exceptions. For example, between New York, Boston, and Washington, it's more or less taken for granted that you'll use the air shuttle, where no reservations are required; you go out to the airport and board the next plane. Your secretary can easily find out. If in doubt, always specify tourist class, and you'll irritate no one. Most business trips are so short these days because of jet speeds that cost-conscious controllers are reluctant to authorize the expense of first class.

In my early executive days, more than 15 years ago, I had gone to California on a particularly strenuous and difficult business trip. It was in the days of the now extinct DC-6, before the days of nonstop flights, and a Los Angeles–New York flight then took as long as 12 hours. Late one afternoon, my supervisor in New York phoned that an urgent matter required that I be back in my office at 9 A.M. the next morning. Could I get a night flight back?

I immediately made a reservation on TWA, and the reservations clerk asked me if I'd like a sleeper berth. The idea was quite appealing. I had never had an air berth before. I was tired. I was expected to be fresh and alert the next morning. The cost would approximate another one hundred dollars above the regular fare. It was an important trip, and an important meeting back in New York. So I said yes.

I boarded the plane late at night, and there it was. In the middle section of the cabin were four berths, two on each side, as I recall it. I had an upper. I climbed up, undressed, and was sound asleep fifteen minutes after we left the ground. I slept so deeply that I wasn't even aware of our landing and takeoff at Chicago. In the morning, the stewardess knocked to awaken me. I felt marvelous.

But not for long. When I submitted my charge slip for reimbursement, all hell broke loose. The financial department pointed out that company policy permitted tourist class travel only, and they refused to reimburse me. Finally, after considerable negotiation and much persuasion, I swore faithfully never again to commit such a sin, and they agreed "just this once" to give me my money back.

It wasn't a question whether valid reasons existed to justify the expense. There was a definite company policy and that was it. I should have known better.

FOLLOW THE COMPANY POLICIES

If you want to spare yourself this sort of travail, learn your company policies in advance of your first business trip. Other typical company travel policies include use of airport limousines instead of taxis in most major metropolitan areas.

If you're attending a convention or trade show, you're normally expected to stay at the hotel where the meetings will be held. If you're traveling to visit a customer or prospect, where you stay is pretty much up to you. Any commercial (but not resort) hotel in the downtown area, or near where you're visiting, is acceptable.

Your secretary should always make reservations in advance at the same time she arranges for your plane tickets. Most likely, a hotel at your destination will be represented in your home city by another hotel in the same chain, and they'll quickly confirm your accommodations. This is much easier than writing ahead for reservations; if space is unavailable, you may discover only when you arrive that you have no place to sleep. Also, be sure your secretary advises the hotel the time you're expected to arrive, so the room will be held for you.

WHAT TO CHARGE THE COMPANY FOR YOUR TRIP

If your company hasn't prepared a written policy on travel expenses, here are some rules taken from one corporate policy manual: "Reasonable" allowance will be paid for meals, valet and laundry charges, tips, and taxis or car rentals when used for business. The company won't reimburse you for the expenses of entertaining yourself for a night on the town or for a sightseeing expedition.

You should be prepared to turn in receipts for your hotel bill and car rental. No one expects restaurant receipts for your meals, but if you're using a credit card, charge slips should be submitted too on your return.

As to the amount of your charges, recognize that you're not the first man the company ever sent to Chicago or anywhere else. Your boss, or the controller's department, has the experience of dozens of other people's trips as a yardstick of comparison. Honesty is the best policy: Charge every penny you spent on behalf of the company, neither more nor less.

WHEN YOUR WIFE SHOULD COME ALONG

At some conventions, your wife's attendance is expected, and in such cases, the program chairman usually plans a separate program for wives during the day. But companies seldom will assume the costs of transporting your wife to a convention. So if you're considering taking your wife along (ah, glorious Chicago!), first ask your supervisor his opinion. You can be reasonably certain the company has a policy on this too, whatever that policy may be.

If the boss says, "Yes, take her along if you wish, but at your own expense," the customary procedure is to make plane and hotel reservations for her at the same time, and in the same manner, as you make your own. If you do this through the company, ask them to tell you the additional charge so that you can reimburse the company. (This is more practical than making your wife's reservation separately; she may be entitled to travel at reduced fares under the family plan.)

The usual convention routine will take your wife away from the business sessions during the day for sight-seeing trips and shopping expeditions. Often wives are invited to attend dinner meetings and late afternoon cocktail parties. Particularly if the dinner is a more formal or important occasion, she should attend, to see and be seen by your colleagues and associates. Attendance at the cocktail parties is optional, because in the alcoholic haze which usually surrounds such occasions, hardly anyone is likely to notice her presence or absence. If she thinks she'd enjoy the party, she should go. If she'd be bored, she should do whatever else she prefers.

Chapter 11

THE JOB OF YOUR SECRETARY

IF YOU'RE EXPERIENCING the satisfaction of having a secretary for the first time in your brief business career, you may not be quite sure what the correct relationship with her should be. I think it's one where, in a pleasant way, she provides you with the maximum assistance to meet your work pressures. Obviously, if there's tension between you, if she dislikes you or *vice versa*, the relationship isn't very good.

Your secretary is there to help you, paid by the company for that purpose. And help you she should. This may include opening your mail, typing your dictation, making your business travel arrangements, arranging your appointments, serving your morning coffee, and many other things. But her duties shouldn't include paying your personal bills, balancing your checkbook, shopping for your wife (or for you). Don't make problems for yourself by asking her to perform these chores. She may do them, but you can be certain she'll resent it.

If you "inherit" a secretary in your new position,

everything you do—or don't do—will be compared to the acts of your predecessor. Sometimes your new secretary will make the comparison mentally. Other times she may come forth with statements like, "Well, Mr. Vance used to give me all of *his* dictation in the morning." It can be very irritating.

She may have helpful suggestions, or they may be valueless, but you want her to realize she's now working for you, not for your predecessor. And you don't like the idea of her measuring you against Mr. Vance. Nor should you.

The best thing to do is to tell her so, tactfully but quickly. You might say, "That's a good suggestion, Miss Atkinson, but we all work differently, and this is *my* way of doing it." If she persists, next time you might say, "Miss Atkinson, I know every secretary operates differently, and I operate differently from Mr. Vance." Don't put yourself in a defensive position; there's no reason for you to follow your predecessor's working habits for the greater convenience of Miss Atkinson— unless you prefer it that way.

KEEP YOUR DISTANCE

Your secretary is your business assistant. If your wandering eye looks at her primarily as a woman instead of as an office associate, you're presenting her with a built-in excuse to get away with second-rate work. If you want a private affair, most experienced executives suggest you have it anywhere but in the office, and, above all, not with your secretary. I knew one fellow who discovered that the only way he could control his impulses was to choose a homely, matronly lady for the post.

However you do it, it's wise to keep a certain proper distance between your secretary and yourself. She should always, without exception, address you as "Mr." Simply because it keeps your relationship on a business-like basis.

Most secretaries these days, however, are addressed by their first names, and they seem to prefer it that way. Just to be sure yours prefers it so, you might ask her, on the day she begins work. (I had one teen-age secretary some years ago who insisted on being called "Miss Cantwell." Her formality puzzled me since she was only one step removed from being a teeny-bopper. But since she wanted it that way, it was O.K. with me.)

STAYING OUT OF HER PERSONAL LIFE

You may find it necessary to prevent your secretary from overstepping the bounds of propriety. Just as you shouldn't inflict your personal problems onto her, she shouldn't bring her private problems to you. An executive in Philadelphia, an old friend of mine, was driven almost wild by a secretary who insisted on telling him every time she had a fight with her boy friend. "Well," I told him, "you're encouraging her by listening. The more you listen, the more she'll talk."

"But am I not supposed to show that I care, that I'm interested in her as a human being?" he inquired.

"Of course you care," I said. "But where do you draw the line? How much do you care? You're not her father. You're her boss." After this and another dozen conversations like it, the next time she began getting involved, he said quietly, "I'm very much interested, Miss Bussie, but we've got a lot of work to do now." And without further discussion, he proceeded to begin dictating. Miss B. made three or four subsequent attempts to bring up her problems of the heart, but each time he quickly turned to his work. In due time, she got the point.

WHEN—AND HOW—TO GET YOUR SECRETARY TO WORK ON TIME

The list of my own secretaries over the years stretches like a parade into distant memory. They have been extraordinarily competent women, conscientious and devoted to their responsibilities. Yet when I recollect my occasional problems with them, the problem of punctuality heads the list. Some of them just couldn't seem to get to work on time. If my experience is typical, you may be struggling with the same problem. When you're ready to begin work, and your secretary hasn't yet shown up, it can become quite frustrating.

Anyone is willing to be understanding and patient about an occasional lateness or indisposition. But continual lateness can disrupt your working routines. It's worth trying to prevent. The first place to try is at the initial interview. You owe it to the young lady—and to yourself—to tell her exactly what the working hours will be, and that you will need her to report for work on time. If she doesn't think she can be prompt each morning, now is her time to tell you.

The first time she appears late, she'll be ready with a prepared explanation and apology. You can quietly tell her you needed her because you had some work to get out. The second time, in a voice dripping with patience, you can explain to her that you understand things sometimes happen that can cause lateness, but you need her at her desk promptly each morning. After a few warnings in this vein, it's time to evaluate whether the inconvenience to you resulting from her lateness outweighs the value of her work for the remainder of the day. Only you can make that decision. Even if you decide to keep her, I would not relax your admonitions.

And if the lateness grows more frequent, perhaps you should consider changing your mind and finding a secretary who can be available when you need her.

OFFICE "COLLECTIONS"—AND YOUR ROLE

In some large offices there has developed the rather quaint custom of making "voluntary" collections for such causes as Linda's forthcoming wedding, Diana's shower, or even for a Christmas gift to the boss. One of the more enthusiastic young ladies makes the round of the secretaries and invites their gifts. Sometimes she starts the ball rolling by placing a dollar bill conspicuously in an envelope to suggest the "proper" amount of the desired gift. This may be going on in your office right now and you don't know about it, because she'd never ask you, or any of the men, to contribute.

But it's a reasonable guess that most of the young women are contributing their dollar every time around, some because they really want to, and others because they would be embarrassed by declining. Torn between loss of part of their income and loss of their pride, they usually prefer to sacrifice part of their income.

Of course, the young lady who organizes these "charitable" endeavors has the best of intentions and is completely honest; the money is actually spent as she promises it will be. But it's unfair because of the strong ingredient of pressure involved. It reduces the girls' take-home pay as effectively as a pay cut. And you're the only one who can stop it. If you discover this is going on in your department, either report it to your own supervisor or, if you're in a position to act on your own, you might circulate a gently worded interoffice memo explaining that despite the worthiness of the causes, the collections have gotten out of hand and must stop immediately. And the fair lassies will regard you as a hero.

WHEN YOUR SECRETARY IS ABSENT

When your secretary is absent or on vacation, courtesy suggests special efforts to ease things for her temporary replacement. Ask your regular secretary to prepare a few pages of essential facts. For example, "Typewriter ribbons are in the third drawer of the filing cabinet. If the typewriter breaks down, call 685-4901. To order coffee, phone 393-4801." And so on. In my office, these informal notes run only a few pages in length, and are in a separate folder where the temporary secretary can find them readily.

HOW TO "LEND OUT" HER SERVICES

Occasionally, one of your colleagues may need some rush help, and you may wish to volunteer the services of your secretary to provide it. But don't let him ask your secretary directly. Instead ask your secretary, in his presence, to help him on the project. Otherwise she may regard his request as an infringement or an imposition. If you doubt it, just try to find a secretary who's willing to work for two men.

Chapter 12

IT'S WISE TO separate your personal life from your business life. Most companies don't care what you do with yourself after office hours (short of grossly offensive behavior or criminal acts). And that's the way it should be.

When you work closely with other men over a long period of time, however, you get to know them quite well. Sometimes you may wish to invite them and their wives to your home for dinner and a social evening. If they're on the same level in the company as you, such an invitation is considered quite proper.

INVITING THE BOSS TO DINNER

It's another story, however, when it comes to inviting your supervisor. In the first burst of cordiality with your new boss, particularly if his age is similar to yours, you may find yourself possessed of the impulse to invite him and his wife to your home for dinner. After all, it would give you the opportunity to get to know him better, and would impress him with your pretty wife and attractive home.

You also know that after you've entertained him and his wife in your home, he may find it difficult to treat you objectively and fairly, and to criticize you if necessary, thereafter. So he may grope for some polite excuse to decline your "generous" invitation. All in all, I think it's better not to create the problem by extending the invitation.

It's entirely possible, however, that your boss may accept your invitation out of friendliness and respect for you. Or because he doesn't know how to say no without offending you.

If he accepts, be sure to brief your wife about your new job, your boss, and your work so that she can listen and participate intelligently in your dinner conversation. If you fail to brief her, it's unfair to the boss, because he knows it's hardly good manners to discuss business when one person at the dinner table doesn't know what he's talking about. And, needless to say, it's hardly fair to your wife.

SPEAK FOR YOURSELF, JOHN

If he shows no inclination to mention the office, then I wouldn't be the one to raise the subject. To some men, business is their whole lives; to others, it's a subject to be avoided during social occasions. Let your boss give you the cue. And guide your wife beforehand. More than one overambitious and undersensitive wife has lured the boss into a corner, told him what a great man her husband is, and pointedly asked the boss about his chances for a promotion. Nobody, including bosses, likes to be boxed into a corner. Such pressure from your wife comes under the "boxing into a corner" heading. It will certainly embarrass and annoy your superior, and when you hear about it after the boss and his wife have left for home, it should embarrass you too. It needn't happen with a little advance warning to your wife. You can speak for yourself.

As you can see, I think there are perils in entertaining your supervisor. The same holds true in regard to your own staff, the people who report to you. If one of them invites you, the easiest way to handle it is to say, "Thanks, I'd like to accept, but our social plans are pretty full right now. Maybe we can do it sometime later on."

As an executive, you want to keep your independence of action. You want to be free to make the decisions you think are best. And you can hardly do that if you're socially beholden to some of the members of your own staff.

DATING IN THE OFFICE

Many companies—perhaps most—prohibit husband and wife from employment in the same department or division. Other companies allow it only if both were employed by the company before their marriage. But no company that I know of encourages a man and woman in the same department to date conspicuously. When your social relationships become a matter of general office gossip, they intrude on efficient and businesslike relationships. If you want to date the blonde down the hall, therefore, office etiquette suggests that you restrict your courting to after-work hours. The office is hardly the place for long, tender, and intimate conversations, whether over the interoffice telephone or at the side of her desk. The ideal office romance is one in which announcement of wedding plans comes as a total surprise to the entire staff; they had never even seen you talking together.

Chapter 13

ASKING FOR A PROMOTION

WHEN A BETTER position opens up within your department, and you want it, a plan of action is called for. You may think you're the obvious choice for the promotion. In fact, you may be the logical choice, but it may not be quite apparent to your supervisor. You can seldom do any harm by a quiet visit to your supervisor, telling him that since Mr. Hudson's position has opened up, you'd appreciate consideration because you believe you could do an outstanding job for the company. That's enough. You don't need to say more, unless there's some aspect of your experience that specially qualifies you and that he might not happen to know.

With that single exception, there's usually no reason for you to attempt to sell yourself. The boss already has observed a good deal about you and your work. It would be difficult for you to go beyond a simple expression of interest without defensively trying to convince him how good you are. That wouldn't become you, and it usually won't help you get the job. The most important thing is to emphasize how the company will benefit from your promotion. The boss is necessarily more concerned with what's best for the company than with you.

INVOLVEMENT IN COMMUNITY ACTIVITIES

Young executives on the rise long ago discovered that a surefire way to gain a favorable reputation in business is participation in community activities, ranging from the Rotary Club and the Jaycees to the United Fund and the Urban League. Such activity exposes a man to the scrutiny of men from other companies. Many a "comer" won his first notice by such constructive work. In other industries, men have found their key in their trade or professional association.

Almost every corporate management wants to be represented in such activities. But protocol is involved. Some companies assign executives of a particular level to represent them. In the case of professional organizations, many companies encourage membership by agreeing to pay part or all of the membership dues and expenses.

This, however, is one area where the young executive should tread carefully. If there's a business organization you'd like to join, don't make a move without first checking with your supervisor. Ask him whether there's a company policy on the subject. And be guided accordingly. If he answers you sullenly, "You're free to join anything you wish," I'd be careful. He may be indicating resentment that you'll attract attention he himself would like to receive but has done nothing to earn. If he encourages you, go right ahead. But if not, it's hardly worth incurring his ill will.

WHEN YOUR RIVAL IS HOSTILE

I've been emphasizing in this book how, when, and why you should be courteous and considerate in business situations. But etiquette doesn't start and end with you. It also depends on the other fellow.

What happens, for instance, if one of your peers, perhaps another young man at the same level on the corporate organization chart, acts discourteously to you? It may be nothing more than failure to respond to your routine "Good morning." Or he may speak harshly, or use curt words in talking with you. You're puzzled what to do about it, because, as far as you know, you've done nothing to deserve it. And you don't like being treated in this fashion.

The best first step is to do nothing. His irritability may be caused by something else entirely that has nothing to do with you. You might watch to see how he talks to others in the office. If he's generally unpleasant to all, then leave him alone; say nothing; he'll hang himself without your help.

If, however, you discover that you are the special target of his hostility, try to figure out why. Perhaps you unintentionally offended him by some past remark. Or perhaps you yourself introduced a note of rivalry into the relationship. If you have reason to suspect this may be the case, I wouldn't apologize or refer to it again, but thereafter would make a special effort to show him friendliness. Very often in these situations, this is all that's needed to eliminate friction, because he may feel defensive toward you.

Sometimes this doesn't work. The man we're talking about may be a ruthlessly competitive fellow who knows realistically that he can win promotion only by knocking you out of the running. He can't find a single reason why he should be gentlemanly to you. If you diagnose the situation in this way, then be prepared to act. Don't make the first move. Wait until his next display of discourtesy, and then say to him quietly but very firmly, "Now look here. If you want to talk to me, please do it in a proper tone of voice." Then turn quickly on your heel and walk away. It's your way of showing that you won't take any nonsense. And your quiet voice demonstrates that you are fully in control of yourself, your emotions, and the situation.

HANDLING A RIVAL—THE GENTLEMANLY WAY

Let me say just a few words about the courteous and gentlemanly way to handle the rival who wants, in the immortal words of Eliza Doolittle in *My Fair Lady,* to "do you in." I won't say much because I've already written two books on the subject.*

Burger's Law (I invented it) says that "you have the right to fight for your own survival." Not everybody agrees with this. Some men think that when you're under attack the gentlemanly thing is to say nothing and do nothing to defend yourself against the dastardly rival across the hall. That is not my theory.

But if you're going to defend yourself, you must know how. Do it like a gentleman. Don't get down in the gutter with your rival. The rules are simple.

Rule 1. Don't complain to your supervisor that you're being attacked. It's your problem, not his.

Rule 2. Don't complain to your colleagues or associates that your rival is seeking your scalp. You don't know which of them may be in your rival's corner. I heard last week of a man who was severely criticized by his boss, and who, shaken, told his assistant all about it. Little did he know that the assistant, seeking his job, was the one who had complained about him to the boss.

Rule 3. Never criticize your rival in personal terms. Personal rivalries don't belong in an office. If you attack your rival in personal terms, you won't look good.

Rule 4. If you have valid complaints to make about

* *Survival in the Executive Jungle,* Macmillan, 1964; *Executives Under Fire,* Macmillan, 1966.

your rival, present them in terms of the damage to the company which his actions or inactions are causing. If he's merely attacking you, nobody will be concerned.

Rule 5. Understate. Keep cool. Don't report disaster when he makes some minor misjudgment. Stick to the facts. Your supervisor may soon come to recognize that your rival's ardor to oust you may have clouded his otherwise sound judgment.

That's enough. You take it from there. Just remember: nothing ungentlemanly. No bare knuckles.

WHEN YOUR BOSS DISLIKES YOU

If you harbor the disturbing suspicion that perhaps your supervisor dislikes you, similar self-control is required.

You may get the word indirectly, in "water-cooler gossip" or you may somehow sense an unfriendliness or curtness of manner; or you may encounter quite direct criticism from your boss.

Almost everyone has experienced such a situation at one time or another. Don't panic. First, make sure you're not imagining things. Maybe the alleged unfriendly sign is nothing more than his failure to compliment you. That hardly proves he's trying to oust you. But if you're certain he is unfriendly, the next step is to figure out why. This is where many men go wrong. They look for the wrong reasons. They wonder if their work isn't good enough. But has one of your actions been an irritant? Like frequent lateness? Or argumentativeness? Or failure to check certain decisions in advance, because you were anxious to demonstrate your fine independent judgment? Or unwarranted aggressiveness? It could be any one of these, or several.

Most often, however, it boils down to one thing: You haven't treated him like the boss. It may be your manner, your tone of voice, how you address him.

Whatever it is, he senses it, and he resents it. He wants to feel that you respect his position (and him). If this description fits your boss and you, you can determine consciously to change your attitude. You can be quite sure that soon thereafter his will change accordingly. It may take a little while, but it will happen.

WHEN TO STAND UP FOR YOUR RIGHTS

In your desire to please the boss and be well liked, you are willing to be reasonable, flexible, considerate, and to accept criticism. But there's a point beyond which you should not go. Perhaps you should draw the line at deliberate and repeated insults to your dignity and self-respect (real, not imagined). One man I know quit his company when he discovered his boss was tape-recording all incoming phone calls. Another left after one week on the job when his boss listened to a business conversation on an extension telephone, interrupted his talk with a customer, and corrected him in a nasty manner. The first time it happened, the employee went in to see his supervisor immediately afterward and said he'd be willing to take criticism, but not over the phone in a humiliating manner. The boss apologized, did it again the next day, and that's when the employee threw up his hands and walked out.

It's easy enough to quit a job dramatically. It takes courage. But sometimes it takes more courage to decide to go home over the weekend and think it over calmly before making up your mind. The terrible "morning after" sometimes doesn't have to happen at all. Perhaps Friday's indignity may appear by Monday morning as nothing more than an impulsive act of tactlessness. Discretion is the better part of valor in the office too. Once you've quit, you can hardly return and ask for the job back. So be certain the indignity you've suffered justifies your self-imposed dismissal.

Chapter 14

IN JAPAN, ONCE you're hired, your job is usually yours for life. This also holds true in other countries where business is conducted along more traditional lines. But in our country, firing is an inescapable part of corporate life. Sooner or later, at some time in your working life, either you'll get fired or you'll have the task of firing a member of your staff. Neither is pleasant to contemplate. But because there is almost an inevitability to the problem, it's worthwhile to think now how you'd handle either contingency when and if the time comes.

Dismissal is a painful experience for the man affected. It's the ultimate rejection. It says to the man, in effect, "You're not good enough to work with the rest of us." Thus, it damages his opinion of himself. It threatens his economic security. It always brings an added strain to a marriage, and frequently that strain is more than an already tenuous relationship can bear.

HOW TO FIRE AN EMPLOYEE

If you've been assigned the job of swinging the ax, you should recognize the devastating consequences of the act and be guided accordingly. You should do it with as much kindness and mercy as possible. That means sparing the victim any further pain, and, if possible, helping him at the same time.

Since dismissal is the ultimate criticism, you can only pour salt on his wounds by giving the victim a detailed explanation of why he's being terminated. The more you explain, the more he'll need to defend himself, because he can't accept your criticism as valid without damaging his opinion of himself. There must be some men who can face that painful reality, but I haven't yet met them. So, in self-defense, he'll probably argue that it's your fault, or the company's; not his. Nobody can win such an argument, and blood may flow.

If you believe that your honest and objective criticism will help him avoid the same consequences next time, I advise you to save your breath. Feeling desperately on the defensive, anxious to protect himself from hurt, he'll close his mind to your "helpful" suggestions. An appropriate quotation is, "I can protect myself from my enemies, but God protect me from friends like this!" This isn't the time to try to be helpful in such a fashion.

You can be more helpful, I believe, if you avoid making things worse than they are. You can avoid further damage to his already battered head if you mask the reasons in polite generalities, or even white lies.

"I'm sorry, but it just didn't work out." Or, "You tried very hard, but this just wasn't the right job for you." "You're a good man, and you did a good job, but our plans have changed, and the job isn't there any more." If he presses you for specifics, you might say, "There aren't any. I've told you everything I can. We're sorry we have to lose you, but I have confidence in you, and I know it's for the best."

IF YOU'RE BEING FIRED

If you're the unfortunate man on the receiving end, a similar approach is recommended. Your objective should be clear in your mind: to do what's best for you. If it were best for you to pour out all your invective on the boss, then I'd recommend your doing it. But it isn't. It brings on lingering death. Sooner or later, whether in a week, three months or a year, some prospective employer will call your boss for references. If you leave the company with an unpleasant name-calling scene, your boss will hardly be disposed to speak kindly of you. He doesn't like the job of firing you to begin with, and an unpleasant scene will only add to his discomfort.

What you want from your boss is, at best, a favorable recommendation, and at the very least, a neutral evaluation. The easiest way to get it is to avoid criticizing your boss as your final act with the company. For instance, you might say, "Mr. Wood, of course I'm sorry this happened. I've liked it here, and I hoped to stay. But I understand these things happen, and even though I don't like it, I know it's one of the things in life I've got to accept. I want to thank you personally for being decent about it."

This won't be easy to do. You're angry as hell. What are you thanking him for? Damn it, he hasn't been decent.

Calm down. Just remember your objective: to get the best possible reference from the man who is firing you. When the time comes, he can say, if he wishes to hurt you, "We had to terminate his employment. His work was unsatisfactory." Or he can say, if he feels kindly, "We had to let him go. He's a good man but he was in the wrong job." Which he says depends on you. And on what he says may depend your future career. So think twice before you decide to blow your stack.

Isn't that the whole point of executive etiquette? It's not an artificial set of rules somebody decided you should follow, but rather a common sense way of making life pleasanter and advancing your own best interests.